CONVERSATIONS
WITH GLENN GOULD

CONVERSATIONS

by Jonathan Cott

LITTLE, BROWN AND COMPANY · BOSTON · TORONTO

FIRST EDITION

LIBRARY OF CONGRESS CATALOGING IN PUBLICATION DATA

Cott, Jonathan.
  Conversations with Glenn Gould.

  Discography: p.
  Filmography: p.
  1. Gould, Glenn. 2. Pianists — Canada — Interviews.
I. Title.
ML417.G68C7 1984   786.1'092'4 [B]   84-12230
ISBN 0-316-15777-5
ISBN 0-316-15776-7 (pbk.)

Sarah Lazin Books

Some of the material in this book was first published, in slightly different
form, in *Rolling Stone* magazine on August 15 and August 29, 1974,
and in *Forever Young* (Random House/Rolling Stone Press, 1977).

The discography was first published in slightly different form in *The
Piano Quarterly*, Fall 1981, No. 115, and is reprinted with the permission of the magazine. Many of the radio and video listings are
courtesy of the Canadian Broadcasting Corporation. All rights in the
photographs provided by the Estate of Glenn Gould are reserved by
Glenn Gould Ltd. and the Estate of Glenn Gould.

The quote from Basho is from *The Sea and the Honeycomb*, edited by
Robert Bly. Copyright © 1971, by Robert Bly. Reprinted by permission
of Beacon Press.

BP

*Published simultaneously in Canada
by Little, Brown & Company (Canada) Limited*

PRINTED IN THE UNITED STATES OF AMERICA

ACKNOWLEDGMENTS

For their help in supplying backmatter and photographs, I would like to thank Stephen Posen of the Gould Estate, Ruth Pincoe and Helmut Kallman of the National Library Archives in Ottawa, Robert Sunter of the Canadian Broadcasting System, Robert Silverman of *Piano Quarterly*, and Stephanie Franklin, our photo researcher.

I am grateful to Paul Scanlon, who shaped these interviews when they first appeared in *Rolling Stone*, and to Jann and Jane Wenner for their support and encouragement. For the preparation of this volume, I thank Patty Romanowski and Sarah Lazin of Sarah Lazin Books, and my editor, Beth Rashbaum, at Little, Brown & Company. Thanks also to Allan Horing and Susan Koscis.

Jonathan Cott
February 1984

CONTENTS

INTRODUCTION

Only as the genius in the act of creation merges
with the primal architect of the cosmos can he
truly know something of the eternal essence of
art. For in that condition he resembles the
uncanny fairy tale image which is able to see
itself by turning its eyes. He is at once subject
and object, poet, actor, and audience.

— NIETZSCHE: *The Birth of Tragedy*

"THE nut's a genius," the conductor George Szell once remarked after attending a performance in Cleveland by the Canadian pianist Glenn Gould.* Since 1947, when he first publicly performed Beethoven's Fourth Piano Concerto at fourteen, Glenn Gould continually amazed and astonished audiences, critics, and professional colleagues alike. He was called a musician of "divine guidance" and the greatest pianist since Busoni. He was also castigated for (1) his unconventional performing mannerisms — loping onstage like a misplaced eland with unpressed tails, sometimes wearing gloves, playing almost at floor level on a sawed-down, short-legged, wooden folding chair and conducting, humming, singing, combating and cajoling and making love to his piano as if it were Lewis Carroll's Snark ("I engage with the snark / Every night after dark / In a dreamy, delirious fight"); (2) his uncompromisingly imaginative choice of repertoire (William Byrd, Bach, Hindemith, and Schoenberg instead of Chopin and Rachmaninoff . . . and more Rachmaninoff); (3) his obsessive search and preference for a tight-actioned piano, meant to facilitate a musical approach that emphasized clarity of definition and textures and a rarely equaled analytical subtlety and acuity — as well as for certain startling but revelatory interpretations of such "standards" as the Brahms First Piano Concerto. (When Gould first performed this piece with Leonard Bernstein and the New York Philhar-

*See Appendix for an account of this incident as well as selected discography, filmography, and listings of radio and television programs.

monic, for instance, Bernstein — with the pianist's ap-
proval — got up before the audience to disassociate himself gently from Gould's approach, which featured slow
tempi and a profound structural design that, for the first
time I could remember, truly revealed the work's pent-up
emotional rapture.)

And finally, Gould was criticized for his eccentric and
hermetic life style (the pianist refused to fly, liked taking
car trips by himself to the far north of Canada, and spent
most of the last half-dozen years of his life sequestered in
a claustral hotel studio on the outskirts of Toronto); for
his bizarre getup (gloves, mittens, T-shirt, shirt, vest, sweater,
coat, and scarf, all in warm weather); and, to cap it all
off, for his having retired, at the wizened age of thirty-
two, from any and all public concert recitals.

Gould's retirement, in fact, allowed him to try to realize
and make good his claims that the functions of concerts
had been — or would soon be — taken over by electronic
media and that it was the recording medium itself that
allowed for an unparalleled analytic clarity, immediacy,
tactile proximity, and catholicity of repertoire. The "analytic dissection by microphone" enabled Gould to present
the music from a "strongly biased conceptual viewpoint,"
just as it permitted the music to emerge with an untram-
meled force and luminescence. As Gould's recorded performances demonstrated, structural clarification always
released new energy.

After his retirement from the stage in 1964, Gould con-
tinued to produce one extraordinary album after another.
(See Discography.) And he interspersed his unsurpassed
Bach realizations with "first" recordings of Richard Strauss's

Gould with conductor Leonard Bernstein at a 1957 recording
session in New York City. *(CBS Records)*

Enoch Arden (accompanying the actor Claude Rains, who recited Tennyson's sentimental, drawing-room poem), the Liszt piano transcription of Beethoven's Fifth Symphony, Bizet's *Variations Chromatiques*, sublime piano realizations of virginal pieces by Byrd and Gibbons, and an astonishingly beautiful piano transcription of Wagner's *Siegfried Idyll*.

Along with his transcriptions, Gould also composed. His works included a string quartet Opus 1, written between 1953 and 1955 — an unabashed romantic composition showing the pianist's *fin-de-siècle* predilection for the works of Bruckner and Richard Strauss; *So You Want to Write a Fugue* for vocal and string quartets — a jocular tour de force that was originally recorded in the early sixties by the Juilliard String Quartet for a plastic insert disc in *HiFi/Stereo Review* and later released on *The Glenn Gould Silver Jubilee Album*; and two dazzling cadenzas to Beethoven's C-Major Piano Concerto.

In addition to his recording career, Gould made a number of pathbreaking programs of "contrapuntal radio" for the Canadian Broadcasting Corporation (using voices in trio sonata form and employing the sounds of a train and the sea as a basso continuo); narrated and performed on— and was the subject of — innumerable radio and television programs; and assembled and arranged music for several shorts and feature films.

Throughout his career, Gould also wrote brilliant and provocative lectures, magazine articles, reviews, and self-interviews on such subjects as the forger as hero of electronic culture, Artur Rubinstein, Petula Clark versus the Beatles, Barbra Streisand and Elizabeth Schwarzkopf, Beethoven as the exemplar of a composer whose "professional developmental skills" conflicted with an "amateur's motivic bluntness," and the analytical importance of the "flip-side overlap" (the four-minute demarcation points at the ends of 78rpm records). These essays and articles were an extension of Gould's brilliant and witty liner-note extravaganzas — similar in style and approach to the eighteenth-century *Spectator* and *Tatler* newssheets — in which the pianist informed his listeners of the state of health of his piano; commented on and theorized about a wide range of musical matters; and offered advice to his critics as to how to write about certain of his performances.

In the notes accompanying his recording of Bizet and Grieg piano pieces, for example, Gould explained that Grieg was a cousin of his maternal great-grandfather, thus affording him a not-to-be-begrudged interpretative authority. And the pianist went on to suggest to record reviewers that, since no previous recordings of the Bizet works existed, "for those of you who greet the release with enthusiasm, I should like to propose a phrase such as ' — vividly and forcefully, as only a first reading can, it partakes of that freshness, innocence, and freedom from tradition that, as the late Arthur Schnabel so deftly remarked, is but a "collection of bad habits." ' On the other hand, for those in doubt as to the validity of the interpretation involved, I venture to recommend a conceit such as ' — regrettably, a performance that has not as yet jelled; an interpretation that is still in search of an architectural overview.' "

And on his Liszt-Beethoven album, Gould printed four parody "reviews" of his interpretation of the Fifth Symphony by four of the pianist's most entertaining critical personae: Sir Humphrey Price-Davies of *The Phonograph* magazine, Professor Dr. Karlheinz Heinkel of *Münch'ner Muskilologische Gesellschaft*, S. F. Lemming, M.D., of the North Dakota Psychiatrists Association, and, finally, Zoltan Mostanyi of *Rhapsodya, Journal of the All-Union Musical Workers of Budapest.* (Gould was, incidentally, awarded a Grammy in 1974 for his liner notes to his recording of Hindemith's three piano sonatas.)

When it was suggested several years ago that Gould collect his liner notes, articles, and essays into a book, the pianist replied that if he reread what he had previously written, he would feel compelled to emend, correct, annotate, amplify, and redo everything — so much so that he would wind up with completely new texts! (Many of Gould's original writings have now been collected in *The Glenn Gould Reader,* edited by Tim Page.) The Canadian music critic William Littler further reports that the pianist "took positive pride in the fact that he had to submit the first draft of a two-minute, forty-three-second speech in his radio documentary on Richard Strauss to no fewer than one hundred and thirty-one edits — about one per second." In a certain parlance, one might well say that Glenn Gould was a classic "control freak." As John Lee Roberts, former head of the Music Department of CBC Radio, once stated, Gould "liked to feel he was in total control of himself every instant of his life." And as Dr. Anthony Storr has described the obsessional artistic personality: "Perhaps the most striking feature of the obsessional temperament is the compulsive need to control both the self and the environment. Disorder and spontaneity must be avoided so far as possible, since both appear threatening and unpredictable."

In a sense, Gould set up and organized his personal and professional life like a series of games with intractable rules. But unlike most obsessive types, whose rigidity and lack of humor foreclosed the possibility of spontaneity, the pianist's seemingly restricting games of life allowed him to manifest *exactly* a spontaneous and unpredictable sense of being and creating. In claustral hotel room and recording engineer's control (!) booth, Gould created his *temenos*, his sacred grove — a hidden place where he could *play* and explore his musical and technological obsessions, far from minatory onlookers and an admonishing outside world.

A philosopher once said that if art were to redeem man, "it could do so only by saving him from the seriousness of life and restoring him to an unexpected boyishness." And on the jacket cover of Gould's debut Columbia recording — a 1955 performance of Bach's *Goldberg Variations* — were thirty contact-sheet-size photographs (one per variation), each showing various aspects and expressions of a boyish-looking young man. And taken together, the photos expressed visually the grace, wit, speed, clarity, passion, daring, and almost androgynous beauty of the astonishing performance of a work that, originally intended to while away the nighttime hours of the insomniac eighteenth-century Russian Count Kayserling, awoke all of us to the presence of a musical genius.

"The Sound of Genius" was the phrase with which Columbia Records immodestly designated and advertised its classical-music artists in the late fifties and sixties; but never was it more accurately applied than to Glenn Gould,

whose progress from record to record (and, for those lucky
enough to see him, from concert to concert) created the
kind of excitement that teenagers long ago, in more traditional times, used to feel when anticipating the publication of a new Tom Swift or Nancy Drew adventure book.
For every album that Glenn Gould proceeded to release
gave evidence not only of the possibilities of a more vital
and rewarding pianistic repertoire (as well as the concom-
itant ongoing revelation of Gould's musical personality)
but also of an interpretative audaciousness free from the
preconditioning and preconceptions of all received cultural
canons and performance "norms." Beethoven's last three
sonatas; music by Mozart and Haydn; piano works by Berg,
Schoenberg, and Ernst Krenek; Brahms *Intermezzi*; and
the ongoing Bach recordings — almost every new recording was accompanied by scintillating, Gould-authored liner
notes and ever-changing record-jacket photographs of our
Hero (looking alternately entranced, relaxed, sensual,
dreamy), and each album promised and fulfilled our long-
ing for adventure and discovery.

Gould fulfilled our expectations because he was a musical explorer who revealed as he created his own artistic
path, noticing things on it that few before him had ever
seen because he observed and heard with the eyes and ears
of a child. "Children," the Italian poet Leopardi once said,
"see everything in nothing; adults, nothing in everything."
And with this childlike sense, Gould perceived, for instance, that the inner lines of a William Byrd pavane, a
Bach fugue, a Beethoven bagatelle, a Brahms intermezzo,
a Scriabin sonata, a Schoenberg suite contained their own
beauty and energy — as well as contributing to the integ-

Gould, in his late twenties, during a recording session.
(The National Library of Canada)

rity and power of the whole composition — qualities awaiting the discovery and release that could be conferred only by Gould's special touch magic, a kind of magic that enabled the pianist to connect himself, as well as his listeners, to the roots of artistic creation. And here lies the ultimate Gouldian paradox: by distancing and isolating himself from his audience, he got ever closer to and more in touch with it . . . and by allowing himself undistractedly to enter and surrender himself to his music, he revealed and gave both it and himself totally to us.

A personal note: At the age of thirteen — filled with typical adolescent turmoil and *angst* — I heard Glenn Gould's recording of the *Goldberg Variations* and attained what I took to be a moment of musical, emotional, and spiritual enlightenment. For it was as if the pianist's performance had truly embodied and brought to fruition Nietzsche's conception of art — "that sorceress expert in healing"— about which and whom the philosopher had written: "Only she can turn [our] fits of nausea into imaginations with which it is possible to live. These are on the one hand the spirit of the *sublime*, which subjugates terror by means of art; on the other hand the *comic* spirit, which releases us, through art, from the tedium of absurdity."

Throughout my teenage years, I attended every concert performance by Gould — both as solo recitalist and as guest artist with several orchestras — in the New York City area. I remember, for example, traveling up to Westchester to see the pianist perform Beethoven's *Emperor* Concerto with a makeshift suburban orchestra, whose conductor (may he remain nameless) was so inept that Gould, score

During the 1955 recording of the *Goldberg Variations*.
(CBS Records)

in hand and playing in a semi-crouching position, decided to half-perform and half-lead the stranded musicians, who gratefully took their cues from their keyboard artist guest, while their *chef d'orchestre*, standing on the podium, obliviously went about waving his arms to the sounds of a different drummer (or pianist)!

I also remember being one of three or four privileged observers at a Carnegie Hall rehearsal session of the Schoenberg Piano Concerto (with Dimitri Mitropoulos leading the New York Philharmonic), at which a shoeless Gould in socks emerged from the wings almost *gliding* onto the stage in his stocking feet, wearing a scarf, carrying a bottle of Poland Water, and warming his hands in a basin of hot water in preparation for what turned out to be the most assured and vital performance of this concerto I have ever heard.

In 1960, I was actually invited to meet my hero in the office of a New York City television station where the pianist had come to discuss the possibility of his doing a series of live performance broadcasts (a project that ultimately fell through). Before the meeting started, I was introduced to Gould who, in spite of the summer season, was wearing his customary outer and inner polar garments. The pianist warily held out his hand to me (a practice that the self-protective Gould was known to avoid). I shook it and heard him give a quiet yell, as I quickly withdrew and uttered my deepest apologies. Gould shrugged, smiled, and quickly forgave me — especially so when I told him of my enthusiasm for his recently released album featuring music by Berg, Schoenberg, and Krenek.

In the mid-to-late sixties, living in California, I occasionally wrote the pianist unabashed fan letters that thanked him for his inspiring and revelatory recordings — in particular his six-record *Well-Tempered Clavier* project — and received an occasional note back from him. Then, in 1974, I had the opportunity of talking to Gould on the telephone for six hours over a three-day period, the results of which were published as a two-part interview in *Rolling Stone* magazine. (It is these interviews — with corrections and added and updated material — that comprise this book.) It was, in fact, during these phone conversations that Gould and I became friends — the phone made it easier for the pianist to make contact and keep in touch with people he liked. And after the interviews were published, whenever I found myself answering the phone at some odd hour and hearing someone asking for me in various, strange-sounding accents (German, French, Russian), I knew it was *Herr* Gould, *Monsieur* Gould, or *Gospodin* Gould on the line.

In 1979, the pianist called me one evening and said: "You know, in three years I'll be fifty, and I've been thinking that that would be a good year for me to give up making piano recordings." "You can't *do* that!" I found myself involuntarily pleading with him. "Well," he tried to console me, "I'll have finished recording the complete Bach for keyboard, most of the Beethoven sonatas . . ." "What about the Sonata No. 28 in A, Op. 101?" I asked. "I heard you perform that once in concert, and *no one* has ever done it so beautifully." "Well, I thank you, sir," Gould laughed. "But if I don't get around to recording it, you can come up to Toronto and I'll play it for you here."

That same year I began two years of full-time work on

Recording the *Goldberg Variations* in 1955 *(left)*
and in 1981 *(above). (CBS Records)*

a book, and had to travel everywhere *but* to Toronto, so I missed that promised private recital — and, unfortunately, Gould never did get around to recording Op. 101. But in 1981, the pianist informed me that, for the first time in his career, he had agreed to allow the French director Bruno Monsaingeon to film an entire series of his recording sessions, during which he planned to make a new version of the *Goldberg Variations* for CBS Records. When the album was released in the middle of 1982, I mentioned to a friend that the front jacket photo of Gould was extremely disturbing, for never had the pianist adorned a cover looking so haunted, pained, and sad. (The back jacket photo ominously showed only Gould's piano and his empty, pillowless chair.)

These photographs had been taken in 1982. But a year earlier, as the recording of Monsaingeon's remarkable film makes clear, Gould — balding and bespectacled and no longer the thin and boyish pianist of 1955 — had nevertheless given us the deepest and most joyful Bach interpretation of his career. Supported by and accountable to a simultaneously overarching and underlying musical pulse — inaudible but *felt* — Gould's new *Goldberg* encapsulated and manifested a lifetime's worth of wisdom and understanding about the music of Johann Sebastian Bach, and particularly about what is probably the greatest set of keyboard variations ever written.

On October 4, 1982 — several months after the album's release — Glenn Gould died. He was fifty years old. Although the pianist had made three additional recordings before his death of music by Brahms, Beethoven, and Richard Strauss (albums that — with the exception of the magnificent performances of the Strauss V *Piano Pieces*, Op. 3 — are uncharacteristically gloomy and funereal in tone, approach, and execution), and although Gould had just begun a new career as a conductor (he led a chamber orchestra in a recording of Wagner's *Siegfried Idyll*), I prefer to remember that his last will and testament was also his first — the *Goldberg Variations*, whose opening Aria also concludes this work that, as Gould described it (and, I like to think, his own playing as well) in his almost thirty-year-old liner notes, "observes neither end nor beginning, music with neither real climax nor real resolution, music which, like Baudelaire's lovers, 'rests lightly on the wings of the unchecked wind.' It has, then, unity through intuitive perception, unity born of craft and scrutiny, mellowed by mastery achieved, and revealed to us here, as so rarely in art, in the vision of subconscious design exulting upon a pinnacle of potency."

PART I

Writing about the works of the late-Elizabethan composer Orlando Gibbons, you once observed: "One is never quite able to counter the impression of a music of supreme beauty that somehow lacks its ideal means of reproduction." You've also talked about the "idealized aspects of the works of Bach." And this emphasis on the idea of "idealization" really seems to me to define your approach to music. . . . But perhaps I'm starting off on too abstract a note.

No, it's marvelous, it's an interesting point, and I suppose that if one fed it into a computer, probably that phrase — "ideal means of reproduction" — or some variant of it would turn up very frequently in what I say and write. I hadn't realized it before, but it *is* a preoccupation, and I think it would be interesting to explore why it is.

But let me start out on a very practical level and proceed from there to something more abstract. I was recently talking to a group of educators about the problems concerning the teaching of pianists in institutionalized technical "factories." You see, I think there's a fallacy that's been concocted by the music teachers' profession, to wit: that there's a certain sequence of events necessary in order to have the revealed truth about the way one produces a given effect on a given instrument. And I said: Given half an hour of your time and your spirit and a quiet room, I could teach any of you how to play the piano — everything there is to know about playing the piano can be taught in half an hour, I'm convinced of it. I've never done it and

I never intend to do it, because it's *centipedal* in the Schoenbergian sense — that is to say, in the sense in which Schoenberg was afraid to be asked why he used a certain row in a certain way, saying he felt like the centipede, which doesn't want to think about the movement of its hundred legs because it would become impotent; it couldn't walk at all if it did think about it. And I said: Therefore I'm not going to give this half-hour lesson, but if I chose to, the physical element is so very minimal that I could teach it to you if you paid attention and were very quiet and absorbed what I said and possibly you could take it down on a cassette so that you could replay it later on, and you wouldn't need another lesson. You would then have to proceed along certain rather disciplined lines whereby you observed the correlation of *that* bit of information with certain other kinds of physical activity — you would discover there are certain things you can't do, certain kinds of surfaces you can't sit on, certain kinds of car seats that you can't ride in.

And by this time I was getting a great laugh — they regarded this whole thing as a routine, which it was *not*. I was trying to make quite a serious point, which was: that if this were *done*, you would be free of the entire tactile kinetic commitment. No, *correction* — you would not be free, you would be eternally bound *to* it, but so tightly bound *to* it that it would be a matter of *tertiary* interest only. It would be something that could be "disarranged" only by a *set* of circumstances that would confuse it.

I once talked about such a "set." It involved a time in Tel Aviv — the fall of 1958, in fact — and I was giving a series of concerts on an absolutely rotten piano, the manufacturer of which shall be left unnamed [laughing]. Israel was, after all, a desert country, as they kept explaining to me, and they had desert pianos, understandably enough. I was playing I think eleven concerts in eighteen days, which for Isaac Stern would be like nothing, but for me is very difficult — *was* very difficult, I should say — and I think eight of the eleven were given on this monstrosity.

In any event, one day I was switching programs, which was a real problem, because till then I'd coasted on a kind of tactile memory based on the experience of playing the earlier repertoire, and now suddenly I had to change. I had to do a little practicing, and it was at that moment that things began to run downhill. So on the afternoon of the first of that series of concerts, I'd gone through a miserable rehearsal at which I really played like a pig because this piano had finally gotten to me. I was playing on *its* terms. I had "put it on," as Mr. McLuhan would say, and I was really very concerned because I simply couldn't play a C-major scale properly. I was incapable, apparently, of responding on any terms but those which were immediately presented to me through the medium of that piano.

So I had a car, rented from the Hertz agency in Jerusalem (the idea of which delights me), and I was in any case staying about fifteen miles outside of Tel Aviv at a place called Herzliyya-by-the-Sea (it's an American colony where there are rather nice hotels and you feel as though you're in the San Juan Hilton). And I went out to a sand dune and decided that the only thing that could possibly save this concert was to re-create the most admirable tactile circumstance I knew of. And at that time *that* was in relation to a piano which I still own, though I haven't used it in many years, a turn-of-the-century (about 1895) Chickering — supposedly the last classic piano built in America — classic by virtue of the fact that it had a lyre that looked as if it were off the cover of the old B. F. Wood edition — short, stubby legs and slightly square sides. This piano was the prototype of the piano that I now use for my recordings and the other one that I have in my apartment as well, in that I discovered a relationship of depth of touch to aftertouch, which admittedly had to undergo a considerable amount of modification for a Steinway. It couldn't just be transferred across the board (no pun intended), and both of the pianos that I own were modified along the lines of this turn-of-the-century Chickering.

So I sat in my car in ye sand dune and decided to imagine myself back in my living room . . . and first of all to *imagine* the living room, which took some doing because I'd been away from it for three months at this point. And I tried to imagine where everything was in the room, then visualize the piano, and . . . this sounds ridiculously *yogistic*, I'd never done it before in precisely these terms . . . but so help me it worked.

Anyway, I was sitting in the car, looking at the sea, got the entire thing in my head and tried desperately to live with that tactile image throughout the balance of the day. I got to the auditorium in the evening, played the concert, and it was without question the first time that I'd been in a really exalted mood throughout the entire stay there — I was *absolutely* free of commitment to that unwieldy beast. Now, the result, at least during the piano's first entrance, really scared me. There was a minimal amount of sound — it felt as though I were playing with the soft pedal down, which at times I often do, but without the intention of creating quite so faint-hearted a piano tone.

I was shocked, a little frightened, but I suddenly realized: Well, of course it's doing that because I'm engaged with another tactile image, and eventually I made some adjustment, allowed for some give-and-take in relation to the instrument at hand. And what came out was really rather extraordinary — or at least I thought so. And so, apparently, did a couple of elderly souls who wandered backstage after the concert. One of them was the late Max Brod — the Kafka scholar, who at that time was living in Tel Aviv and who wrote for the Tel Aviv German paper. He came backstage with a lady, whom I took to be his secretary, and made a few nice sounds, and the lady in question, whose name I didn't catch, came up to me and in a rather heavy German accent said — bear in mind I'd just played Beethoven Two — and said [conspiratorial half-whisper], "Mr. Gould, ve haf attended already several of your pairformances in Tel Aviv, but tonight's, zis vas somehow, in some vay, somesing vas different, you vere not qvite one of us, you vere — you vere — your being vas *removed*." And I bowed deeply and said, "Thank you, madam," realizing of course that she had in fact put her finger on something that was too spooky to talk about even, and I realized that with her obviously limited English there was no way I could convey what I'd really done. But then she finished it off by saying, "Yes, I haf just been saying that zis was unquestionably ze finest Mozart I haf ever heard" [laughing], and of course it was Beethoven.

When you were sitting in the car in the desert, were you performing the piece in the air on the dashboard, or . . .

Neither, neither. The secret is that you must never move your fingers. If you do, you will automatically reflect the most recent tactile configurations that you've been exposed to.

Is there a difference between imagining a total performance of a piece and performing it in your imagination? Were you simply imagining a performance of the piece in your mind?

No. That is something profoundly to be wished for and not necessarily contradictory to what we've talked about, but at a certain point there is an overlap, and odd bits and pieces stick out, and I think we should define those bits and pieces. There *is* a difference, and the difference is something like this: I don't know if you've ever experienced it — and certainly they're not going to try it on me — but some years ago they discovered a remarkable method of local anesthesia which was employed in dentistry. The method was that of taking a patient who, for some reason, was reacting badly to Carbocaine or Zylocaine or whatever-ocaine, and giving him two dials, one of which contained white noise, while the other controlled possibly a radio or a cassette or record player, on which was a piece of musical information with which the patient was familiar — Mantovani or Beethoven — whatever he knew. It had to be something he could "pull in," so to speak. Now then, that meant that his reaching out to that source had to be impeded in some way, there had to be an area of *blockage*, and that area of blockage was represented by the dial which controlled the white noise. It was arranged in various ratios, but at all times the ratio of white noise to actual sound had to be in favor of the white noise, so that you had to fight through that sound barrier, quite literally, in order to pull out remnants of a remembered sound. And it was discovered that without exception this was the most effective local anesthetic they'd ever employed in dentistry. They had a remarkable success with it . . . except that there were very few people who were willing to have it tried on them [laughing]. But the reason for its success, I think, is quite obvious: if you are forced to concentrate totally on some object that is other than that which concerns you most deeply at the moment, there's an element of transcendence implied in that concentration.

To give you another example of the same sort of thing: years ago I was playing for the first time Beethoven's Sonata no. 30, Opus 109. I was about nineteen at the time and I used to try out pieces that I hadn't played before in relatively small Canadian towns, and this one fell into a program that I was giving about one hundred twenty miles from Toronto — a university town called Kingston. I never bothered to practice very much — I now practice almost not at all — but even in those days I was far from being a slave of the instrument. I tended to learn the score away from the piano. I would learn it completely by memory first, and then go to the piano with it afterwards — and that, of course, was another stage in the divorce of tactilia from expressive manifestations of one kind or another. No, that's not quite accurate, because, obviously, certain expressive manifestations were built into the analytical concept, but the tactile assumptions were not.

Now, Opus 109 isn't a particularly difficult or strenuous piece, but there is in it one moment which is a positive horror, as you perhaps know, and that is in the fifth variation in the last movement — a moment which is an upward-bound diatonic run in sixths. It's an awkward moment, not only in terms of black-versus-white note fingerings but also in terms of that break in the keyboard around two octaves above middle C where problems of repetition most often show up. For at that point you have to change from a pattern in sixths to a pattern in thirds, and you've got to do that in a split second. I had always heard this piece played by people who, when that moment arrived, looked like horses being led from burning barns — a look of horror would come upon them, and I always wondered what was so intimidating about it.

Anyway, about two or three weeks before I was to play the thing for the first time, I started to study the score, and about a week ahead of time I started to practice it (which sounds suicidal, but that's the way I always operate). And the first thing I did, foolishly — very bad psychology — was to think in terms of: Well, let's try the variation, just to make sure there's no problem — it had never *seemed* to be one when I sat down and read the thing through when I was a kid . . . but better try it, better work out a little fingering system just in case, you know. And as I began to work out my system, one thing after another began to go wrong. Before many minutes had elapsed I found that I'd developed a total block about this thing. And three days before the concert, the block, which I'd tried to get rid of by all kinds of devious means — not playing the piece at all, for instance — had developed apace, so that I couldn't get to that point without literally shying and stopping. I just froze at that particular moment.

I thought, something's got to be done about this — I've got to change the program or delete the variation or pretend that I know something about the autograph that they don't. So I decided to try the Last Resort method. That was to place beside the piano a couple of radios, or possibly one radio and one television, turn them up full blast — that's really in effect the experiment that years later I was to read about re Non-Anesthetic Dentistry — turn them up so loudly that, while I could feel what I was doing, I was primarily hearing what was coming off the radio speaker or the television speaker or, better still, both. I was separating, at this point, my areas of concentration, and to such an extent that I realized that *that* in itself would not break the chain of reaction. (It had already begun to make its mark, the problem had begun to disappear. The fact that you couldn't hear yourself, that there wasn't audible evidence of your failure, was already a step in the right direction.) But I realized that I had to do something more than that.

Now, in this variation, the left hand has at that moment a rather uninspired sequence of four notes, the third of which is tied over the bar line. There's not too much you can do with those four notes, but I thought — all right, there are, we'll say, in terms of accent and so on, maybe half a dozen permutations that would be possible [sings several of the permutations], and I played them as un-musically as possible. In fact the more unmusical the better, because it took more concentration to produce unmusical sounds, and I must say I was extremely successful in that endeavor. In any event, *during* this time my concentration was exclusively on the left hand — I'd virtually forgotten about the right — and I did this at varying tempi and kept the radios going, and then came . . . the *moment*. I switched off the radios and thought: I don't think I'm ready for this . . . need a cup of coffee, made a few other excuses, and then finally sat down. The block was gone. And now, every once in a while, just for the hell of it, I sit down and do that passage to see if the block's still gone. It still is, and it became one of my favorite concert pieces.

Now, the point is that you have to *begin*, I think, by finding a way to any instrument that gets rid of the whole notion that the instrument presents you with a set of tactile problems — it does, of course, but you have to reduce those problems to their own square root, so to speak, and having done that, adapt any kind of situation in relation to that square root. The problem then is to have a sufficient advance and/or extra-tactile experience of the music so that anything that the piano does isn't permitted to get in the way. In my own case, my means toward this is to spend most of the time away from the piano, which can be difficult because you occasionally want to hear what it sounds like. But a certain analytical ideal (which is somehow contradictory, I can't quite think how — I'm a bit stupid today, but anyway . . .), an analytical *completeness*, at any rate, is theoretically possible as long as you stay away from the piano. The moment you go to it you're going to diminish that completeness by tactile compromise. Now, at some point that compromise is inevitable, but the degree to which you can minimize its effect is the degree to which you can reach out for the ideal that we were talking about.

A number of pianists have talked about their anxiety dreams in which they continually saw themselves walking out onstage naked or sitting down to find themselves unable to play, like Sparky and his Magic Piano, which refused to perform at the necessary time.

I only have one dream of that kind, which one would think would have abated the moment I stopped giving concerts, but it didn't. I simply transferred it to other media, and I now have it in relation to recording sessions. The dream always makes me aware of the fact that the repertoire that I think I'm doing is not the repertoire I'm really doing. Now in order to make that practical it's never therefore a solo performance; it's usually an orchestral recording, and I've had many variations on this dream.

The most elaborate variation, in fact, took place in an opera house. I was backstage in rather cramped dressing-room quarters, and while wandering around, I saw some-one come up to me — at that time it must have been the equivalent of Rudolf Bing or Rolf Liebermann — and he came rushing up to me, saying: "Mr. Gould, you're just the man we need!"

It turned out that they were going to give a performance of some Bellini opera with Mme. Callas, and the lead baritone had fallen ill or lost his voice, and I was supposed to go on. "This is absurd, I'm no singer." "Of course you are," the man replied, "I mean, you can read a score. You have an innate grasp. . . ." And they threw this score into my hands, and I quickly looked through it, hoping just to grasp the idiom. They told me that they'd describe, as I came offstage, what the next scene would be, and for the rest of it, I'd just have to obey my musical conscience.

Well, I couldn't let them down, could I? I was told that when Mme. Callas was kneeling before an altar — I was at this point standing in the wings — I was to enter stage left, she would greet me, and we'd go into a duet. I surmised she would open it, and she started [Gould sings florid coloratura passage] or something like that. And then I responded with sixths and thirds, "Ya dum, ya da la da leeee da la . . . ," and we were going along *magnificently* with superb euphony. But all of a sudden, a diminished chord, which I thought was heading back to E major, decided to veer off and go to G — as diminished chords have a tendency to do [laughing]. And I was left hanging there. . . . So you can add this dream to your collection of naked moments.

In your striving for the ideal performance, you can often be heard humming and singing, turning some of your solo piano recordings into lieder recitals. I've always felt this was a compensation for the inflexibility and imperfectibility of your instrument. If you could, though, would you try to eliminate this "additional" poltergeist on your recordings?

Oh yes, and if I could find an equalization system that would get rid of it, which I obviously haven't to date — if it occurred at only one frequency, a frequency that would be expendable in terms of the piano — I would cue it out in a second; to me it's not a valuable asset, it's just an inevitable thing that has always been with me. In fact, when I was a kid — really a kid, nine or ten years old, playing my star pieces at student concerts — people said exactly the same thing as they now say about my latest records — so it really doesn't make any difference, I've never been able to get rid of it.

It wasn't until about 1966 or '67 that we started putting a baffle beside the piano, and that has helped a bit. I think if you "a" and "b" any record done now with a record done prior to that time, there's a noticeable improvement. But the other problem, of course, is that since we've moved the whole operation to Toronto we have a drier hall than the one we used in New York, and consequently I think it exaggerates my voice. *Because* it's a drier hall we decided to capitalize on that quality, and we've gone in very close — we always did mike closely, we've never made use of your ideal Deutsche Grammophon concert hall pickup. But in Toronto we've gone in even closer, which I think gives it a very lovely and very clear sound, but it does necessarily augment the voice a little. So there has been a slight increase in the vocal disturbance the last two years [laughing], but it would still not be up to the great old days of pre-1967.

I heard that for one of your first recordings you actually wore a gas mask during the session.

No, I didn't, that was a joke. Somebody brought one in and I put it on, just for the hell of it, and pretended I was going to keep it on. I think Howard Scott, my first producer at Columbia, picked it up at a war surplus store as a gag.

*Your posture at the piano has been the occasion of many
jokes — slouching position, sitting on a chair hardly off
the floor, conducting with your left hand while the right
hand is playing, your nose on the keys, swooning into space,
your whole body totally involved in the musical situation.
Would you change this aspect of your playing if you could?*

No, if I didn't do that there would be an absolute de-
terioration in my playing. That is an indispensable com-
ponent, and for the life of me, I've never seen why anyone
should concern himself with it. The other thing about my
singing is genuinely objectionable for people who lay out
their $5.98 or whatever and say, "Gee, do I have to listen
to that? It may be interesting as a document, but it's an-
noying as sound." Well, I would feel exactly the same
way. In fact, I was just listening the other day to one of
the last records Barbirolli made, the *Pelleas und Melisande*
of Schoenberg (which is a magnificent performance, by
the way), and he obviously got carried away several times.
It doesn't bother me, really, but I can well imagine that
some people will be bothered by it, as they are by Casals's
records, for that matter. I do think it's a valid objection.
But the other business is surely a private matter between
my left hand and my right, and I can't see why it's of
concern to anybody.

There's another thing, of course, that you have to remember, and that is that the caricature of my playing is
that of someone whose nose is touching the keyboard.
Now, in point of fact that happens only under optimum
circumstances in terms of repertoire. It does not happen
as a general rule — not that I sit the rest of the time like

Gould in concert, Moscow, 1957. Gould was the
first Canadian musician to perform in the USSR.
(The National Library of Canada)

Wilhelm Backhaus or whomever. I discovered early on
that there are certain keys to the kingdom in terms of
manipulating the instrument which are not those of the
Prussian school, obviously. The special circumstances in
terms of repertoire have to do with situations that do not
demand a widening of the hands — say, Bach or Mozart
or pre-Bach. But you cannot, you simply cannot play
Scriabin in that position, for the simple reason that the
leverage required to support a widening of the hands is
such that you have to be further away from the keyboard,
you couldn't be that close. But you *can* play Bach that
way, and should, because by so doing you refine the sound,
you minimize the pianistic aspects of it, and you increase
your control — I don't want to be dramatic and say "a
thousandfold," as one of the senators did today (I've been
watching the Watergate hearings all day — I don't know
which senator it was, oh, yes, it was Gurney), but certainly
by a considerable measurement.

And the other factor involved is the nature of the piano
that you use. If you use a piano with a conventional heavy
action and/or a deep action, you're obviously going to have
to make certain adjustments. This brings us, of course, to
another fallacy that piano teachers like to spread about:
there is a notion abroad in the land that you in some way
benefit by learning to play on a difficult instrument, the
theory being that if you can play on a heavy piano, by the
time you get to a light one your task will consequently be
easier. This is as sensible as saying that by learning to play
on a piano it will make you a good harpsichordist. I mean
it does *not* — it does exactly the opposite; it means that
the harpsichord is, in fact, more difficult to play precisely

because you're used to what is, in harpsichord terms, *over-kill.*

In my case there's no problem because I use only one piano and have for the last fifteen years. The piano that I do all my recordings on since 1960 is a piano built in '45 but reconditioned by me in '60 and many times subsequently, including last year, when it had to be completely rebuilt — it was dropped by a truck. Anyway, the long and the short of it is that this piano has a very light action, as indeed all pianos that I prefer do. Many people say it's tinny and sounds like a harpsichord or a fake harpsichord or God knows what. Maybe it does. I think it has the most translucent sound of any piano I've ever played — it's quite extraordinary, it has a clarity of every register that I think is just about unique. I adore it. But, as I've said, it happens to have a very light action. Now if it had a different system of leading, if the draft of the key (which means the fall from top to bottom) were different, if the relationship of the aftertouch to the kickback point when you're depressing a key were different — if any or all of those things were different, one would not be able to sit at that piano as you do. You would have to exert a different leverage and sit further back, of necessity.

But because this conventional wisdom, the origin of which I do not know, began to travel abroad in the early years of this century, it was assumed that the great classic pianos were in some way heavy pianos. The Mason & Hamlin, for instance, was regarded at one time as a classic piano. . . . It *was* a very heavy piano, with beautiful qualities, but it wasn't a piano with the kind of action that I find appealing. That sort of instrument, and/or any other kind modeled after it, poses problems of leverage that would make it very difficult for me to adopt the posture that I would like to.

You haven't only released piano recordings. There are harpsichord performances by you of four of Handel's Suites, as well as a wonderful organ performance of the first part of Bach's Art of the Fugue. *And I've noticed, in these recordings, that you seem to work against the grain of the predominant temperamental characteristics of each instrument. For instance, on the harpsichord, where you can't easily duplicate the arched line and sustained legato of the piano, you seem to aim for just those two qualities. In your piano recordings you aim for the immediacy of attack provided more easily on the harpsichord. And on the organ, you produce a sense of spriteliness more characteristic of both the piano and harpsichord.*

Yes, I think you're absolutely right, there's a kind of cross-fertilization involved here. I'll let you in on a secret, however, in regard to both the organ and the harpsichord records: both of them were done literally without practicing on those instruments at all; my preparation for both was on the piano exclusively. I don't own a harpsichord and never have, and there's only one harpsichord in the world that I can play, and that's one that many pro-harpsichord-ists turn up their noses at — the Wittmayer — simply because its tactilia, and particularly the width of its keyboard, is as close to the piano as one can get. I love it, however, and the particular Wittmayer that I used was owned by a choirmaster here in Toronto who just has it for his own amusement. It's the equivalent of a baby grand, a five- or six-foot instrument, and it lacks certain amenities such as a lute on the four-foot, which I would dearly like to have and which any self-respecting harpsichord offers. Anyway, the registrations for that record were worked out movement by movement as the sessions progressed. I did exactly the same thing with the organ record. Of course, I was somewhat more experienced as an organist because I had played the organ as a kid, but I hadn't played it *since* I was a kid, and again, I set up registrations only at the last minute.

It's part and parcel of the anticipatory syndrome that I've often talked about in relation to conducting. With the harpsichord, of course, one deals with a particular set of tactile problems and a more or less immediate response to their solution, whereas when one conducts, the tactile problems are, in a sense, imaginary, and the response to their solution is delayed — but there are certain parallels nonetheless. On the harpsichord, for example, it's very easy to achieve the sort of secco, pointillistic, détaché line that I've always tried to produce on the piano with varying degrees of success. On the other hand, having achieved it, you can't influence it dynamically and you're left, so to speak, beholden to the generosity of the ear which is sometimes prepared to read dynamic implications into rhythmic alterations. But this introduces another set of problems, because, on the harpsichord, you have a choice between rhythmic inexorability and its converse, which is infinite rubato, a kind of sound-world which really never comes to rest on any bar line. I was determined to try and find a way around that problem. And I thought, well, the best solution would be to pretend that I'm not playing the harpsichord at all [laughing], because if I do otherwise,

I'll fall into exactly the same trap. And I found as the
sessions wore on that that danger was very real indeed
because it's very, very difficult to play a straight, square
eight bars on the harpsichord witout making some rhythmic
alterations in lieu of dynamics. Sometimes indeed I *had*
to do that; sometimes there simply was no other way to
shape a phrase. In very chromatic writing like the beginning of the Variations of the big D-Minor Suite, you have
to do something of the sort. And again in the cadenza-
like Prelude of the A-Major Suite, you've got to differ-
entiate between all those scales and runs — otherwise it
really does sound like a sewing machine. But that aside,
once having hit the stride of a certain tempo, I would like
to be able to hold it almost as tightly as you can on a
piano.

*Don't certain harpsichord pieces need exactly this kind
of rubato approach, like the works of Couperin, for example?*

Oh, yes. I'm sure that's true. But Handel, at least to
me, is a very regal figure and needs a certain kind of
straightforwardness and uncomplicatedness, essentially, as
well as an almost deliberate lack of sophistication, and that
would not be true of Couperin. In any case, the rubato
that one applies to Couperin has more to do with social
grace than structure.

*I once attended two lectures you gave in which you talked
about the nature of the bass line in music. And it seems
to me that your belief in and emphasis on a well-defined
bass line — and also the inner lines of a composition —*

*connects many of your performances . . . not only of Bach
but also of Brahms and Scriabin, and even, as I'll get to
later, of Mozart, where one would not usually expect such
an emphasis. Do you still consider this bass line as seminal
to your conception of music?*

Yes, absolutely. I think that a lot of it has to do with
certain early memories of the way in which one was taught
to analyze music. And I remember those lectures very well
because in each of them there was a centerpiece. In the
first one I discussed the first movement of Beethoven's
Opus 109, which we talked about in another context earlier. And that is a very spooky movement in terms of what
can be made to happen in the imagination as you're playing it and the way in which one changes one's approach
to the notion of structure according to the analytical system
that you choose to employ. (In the second lecture, by the
way, I discussed the first movement of the Bruckner Eighth
Symphony in which I tried to prove pretty much the same
thing.) But the Beethoven was a beauty because, basically,
it's a very simple movement: it simply goes three times
through something that sounds not unlike a chorale except
that it's broken into arpeggiated figures, followed twice
through by what is really just a succession of scales and
arpeggios and flourishes — and it's very, very brief: three
bars plus three bars and a bit of a cadenza. And these
segments were the ones that I was concerned with because
they stand, in the first place, in lieu of the secondary theme
area of a conventional exposition (had there been one,
which there wasn't) and, in the second place, of the re-
capitulation. And what I was showing was the degree to

which absolute as opposed to approximate correspondences existed harmonically.

What I was trying to establish was that, by analyzing these two segments from Opus 109 in a certain way, one could, in fact, determine that Beethoven was actually playing with absent roots, i.e., roots that were not actually sounded in all cases but which produced an absolute mathematical correspondence in those segments. And that what he was really doing was at least as spooky as what one finds in the beginning of the last act of *Parsifal*. It opened up the whole question as to whether Beethoven knew what he was up to or whether it was simply a subconscious process on his part. And the question is: to what extent does the whole process of cerebration really help? Does it matter whether Beethoven knew? And if he didn't know, was it like the question that Schoenberg used to pose about whether the woodcutter, in accidentally producing a fine object, had or had not made a work of art? And in order to attempt to prove that maybe he knew, I exaggerated a little bit — but *only* a little bit — by drawing on the teachings of Sechter . . .

Sechter?

Simon Sechter. He was a theorist and a teacher of Bruckner with whom, believe it or not, Schubert had planned to study just before he died. Schubert at that point had decided that he didn't really know very much about music [laughing], and that it was time that he had some lessons from somebody who did. At least so the legend goes, since I don't know really if that's true or not. At any event, Sechter's approach, which turned out to be seminal in relation to the whole notion of nineteenth-century music and its psychological implications, was that you did not have to sound a root tone for that tone to be psychologically present. And I mean not only in the sense that an inversion of a triad was still that triad in its primary function, or in a close variation of its primary function — I don't believe in that at all — but in the sense that you could have a certain cluster and there would be one note absent from it that was the key to its function as a cluster, the key to where it was going and point from which it had come. And the most obvious example of this, of course, is the opening of *Tristan*. There's also the story of someone criticizing Schoenberg's *Verklärte Nacht*, saying, "Well, it's a very fine student work, Mr. Schoenberg, but you do have a ninth chord with the ninth in the bass in bar thirty-two, and you repeat this in bar 200-and-something-or-other" [laughing]. And it's a chord with B flat followed by A flat a seventh above, followed by C, E flat, G flat, and an additional C thrown in for good measure, resolving into B natural, A natural, D natural, F natural, B natural. . . . Now, Schoenberg, of course, was in his usual fury about this whole thing because to him, any conceivable configurational plan, so long as it remained faithful to a root, present or absent or whatever, was viable and made the situation admissible. Because he was basing his whole analytical precepts on the notion of the absent root.

What does this interpretation have to do with your highlighting the bass lines or the inner lines of a composition?

Oh, yes, right, I forgot to bring it full circle. It's precisely because, not necessarily in the bass line, but in all likelihood at some place other than in the upper line, you will find a moment of focus that is not just there for fun and games — it *is* fun and games too to pull out inner voices, I adore it just for the hell of it . . . I wouldn't deny that for a minute [laughing]. But quite beyond that it seems to me that, structurally, this moment of focus or sequence or whatever it might be relates primarily to something that happens to occur not in the upper voice but rather in some other voice — like the tenor, for example.

Mozart's nonpolyphonic style would seem to be least suited to your temperament, and in fact your version of the C-Minor Piano Concerto has been criticized for your addition of embellishments and a number of continuo passages. You've also released three albums of Mozart piano sonatas — and a fourth is just coming out [since the interview, Gould recorded a fifth album] — and when I first heard them I thought they were a put-on. In fact, they seem to have gotten progressively wilder as the series progresses — Alberti bass lines smashing out, manic or depressive tempi. And then I began to think that perhaps you were taking a Brechtian approach to these works — distancing them in order to get away from the typical emotive type of performances we're used to hearing. But this is a pretty perverse way to deal with Mozart, isn't it?

You're absolutely right, I think, and I'll take it point by point (I can't get John Dean out of my head: "I'll take it point by point if I may, Mr. Chairman"). Let me deal first of all with the C-Minor Mozart. It's the only Mozart concerto that I've recorded because it's the only one that I sort of halfway like. My objection to that record is that

I didn't do nearly *enough* continuo-izing. First of all, those who commented on the things that I added are just plain wrong: It's documentable fact that Mozart himself made it up as he went along, we know that. Not only that, he took it for granted that everybody else would, too. You've got to remember that Mozart was still much-influenced by the concept of figured bass. The Haydn concerti, after all, are full of figured bass ideas, and all other differences to the contrary notwithstanding (differences of orchestration, of length, and so on — the major difference between let us say the earliest of Haydn's concerti and the latest of Mozart's . . . and the C-Minor is one of the late ones) would be that in the Haydn, the soloist was still doubling as a continuo player. Or, he might sit at one harpsichord and do his thing, and the conductor would sit at another harpsichord and support him with some doodlings based on figured-bass notations which amplified the harmonic texture but which were not in themselves absolute.

Now, after thirty years or so, by about 1785, say, the role of the conductor *has* become absolute, or at any rate if not that, the role of the soloist has been at least consolidated into that of one person. But the Mozart keyboard style, in the concertos anyway, is still tied to the preconception of a continuo-style support for the solo instrument. And the solo textures consequently are very thin, very undernourished in the Mozart concerti, they're really very badly written. The unaccompanied moments are beautiful, they're gorgeous, one couldn't have a more beautiful cantilena than the opening of the A-Major Concerto's slow movement — that's a magnificent moment of keyboard writing. But it just so happens that once the orchestra enters (Mozart is a right-handed composer), he literally does nothing with the left hand. And the reason for that is very simple: he was still thinking in terms of that type of concerto, twenty years back, in which the conductor had given continuo support.

Now we get to the sonata recordings. I had more fun with those things than anything I've ever done, practically, mainly because I really don't like Mozart as a composer. I love the early sonatas — I love the early Mozart, period. I'm very fond of that period when he was either emulating Haydn or Carl Philipp Emanuel Bach but had not yet found himself. The moment he did find himself, as conventional wisdom would have it, at the age of eighteen or nineteen or twenty, I stop being so interested in him, because what he discovered was primarily a theatrical gift which he applied ever after not only to his operas but to his instrumental works as well, and given the rather giddy hedonism of eighteenth-century theater, that sort of thing doesn't interest me at all.

There is, as you know, a tradition in Mozart-playing — and you described it beautifully with the word "emotive" — a tradition in which one played with the masculine-feminine "opposites" within the first and usually the last movements of the sonatas. Well, you know the sort of thing I mean: one had that which was stern, that which was melting, that which was commanding, that which was seductive — in opposition to each other. Now, that's all very well and good, except that that whole concept had just begun to go around the symphonic world at the time when Mozart wrote those sonatas. Now, again I seem to be leaning heavily on historical argument, which I don't like to do, because, as I say, I defy it so often that I could be hoisted on my own petard; it's not a safe ground in court for me. But in view of the fact that I lack any other argument at this moment, I will have recourse to it nonetheless.

The plain fact is that the Haydn sonatas, for instance, which are much more extensive in the canon than the Mozart — there being fifty-something to seventeen or eighteen — are also more interesting as pieces, as pieces and as experiments, musically. It's the only late-night music that I've sat down and really played for myself in the last year — well, occasionally Wagner or something like that — but otherwise it's Haydn sonatas, the early ones especially, the baroque-ish ones. They are *so* beautiful and in every case so delightfully innovative. One never gets the feeling that any two are cut from the same cookie stamp. I do get that feeling in Mozart, I'm afraid. I get the feeling that once he hit his stride, they're *all* cut from the same cookie stamp. I think that as Mozart became relatively successful as a theatrical craftsman, his instrumental compositions declined in interest very rapidly.

Now, coming back to what I said about the idea of "opposites": The coalition of opposites was by no means fully developed at that time — it was only in its first stages. (By the time you get to Beethoven, of course, the earliest sonatas already exhibit it in a much more full-blown state, though even there there are some reservations.) But the point is, I think, that if you examine Haydn about the same period, you find that Haydn — who was after all Mozart's god in many ways, certainly in instrumental writing — was not developing this idea as a consistent phenomenon, but in fact toward the end of his life was getting further away from it, so that on occasion, the second theme is also the first theme — there's a kind of Lisztian consistency in the later Haydn sonatas in that a rhythmic configuration will be lifted, from the tonic to the dominant, say — just as Bach might have done in a rondeau or something like that.

But the psychological argument for the arrival of a new moment — a new key, a new theme, whatever — is that one must slow down or soften down or make the phrases legato, as opposed to upright and nonlegato previously, if that's what they were — in other words, a change of heart and temperament. And this doesn't seem to me all that justifiable in the Mozart sonatas.

Indeed, I think the proof of the fact that these developments hadn't *fully* infiltrated the music Mozart wrote in mid-career is that Mozart never really did learn to write a development section, because, of course, you don't have to write a development section unless you've got something to develop. I'm not being flip about that. I mean, literally, that the development section in the classical sonata was there in order to crystallize the potentialities of opposite forces, and it was precisely Beethoven, whose structural notions were based on the coalition of opposites, who wrote developments until you begged for the return to some kind of sobering tonic reaffirmation. And, of course, Haydn also wrote much more extensive developments than Mozart, even though, as I've said, Haydn was not terribly interested in the masculine-feminine coalition. In any case, I really think that the notion that one must start a Mozart sonata with a firm, upright kind of tempo and steady beat and then relax into something that is slurpy and Viennese, and then return to a hint of the original pulse just before the double bar and follow that with a bridge passage and so on, is pretty silly. It's simply not borne out by the music, it really isn't. As I say, I'm reluctant to situate the argument so firmly on some sort of historical pedestal, because I normally am prepared to argue much more eccentrically for the things that I do, but in this case I really can argue that way.

Which brings me to why I had fun with it. I had fun with it precisely because you can play the damn things in the most deliciously straightforward manner, never yielding at a cadence, never giving up for a moment, just going straight through to the end with baroque-ish continuity, if you will. And this has nothing to do with tempo per se. You can do it just as successfully with a slow tempo as with a fast one. Well, not quite as easily perhaps — a slow tempo just by the weight of its duration makes you want to make more curves in the music, that's certainly true. But in any event, such structures can, I think, be made to work without regard to the tempi that you choose.

Now, the horror and the outcry that resulted from my Mozart recordings — I think it was the critic Martin Mayer who said about Volume 2: "Finally, this is madness!" or something to that effect — is to me terribly funny, because all the critics are really responding to is a denial of a certain set of expectations that have been built into their hearing processes. I'm not saying that one can or should try to develop this theory ad infinitum, but there is one thing that's instructive to remember, and that is that if you listen to any decent conductor, and give him the same material appropriately orchestrated, he's not going to stop at the dominant modulation and go into a whole new tempo. He may soften the strings or change their bowings a little, but he isn't going to change the tempo.

I wanted to ask about the famous red herring that almost anyone who doesn't like your playing immediately uses against you — the question of tempo. To me, it seems that the emotional content and structural form of a piece isn't so much determined by a fast or slow tempo, but rather that, in a qualitative sense, whatever tempo you choose creates, within that tempo field, a certain level of tensions and relationships. So that the tempo appears, in a way, like a container into which a liquid is poured.

I couldn't agree more and can't begin to top that in terms of expressing it so well. The best example of that, if we talk about just the classical literature, is Artur Schnabel. I think that Schnabel, and I'm not exactly saying anything new, was probably the greatest Beethoven player who ever lived. I find myself more genuinely drawn to the essence of Beethoven in Schnabel than I ever have been by anybody. I mean, you may not particularly care for the way he did certain things, but by God, he knew what he was doing. There's a sense of structure that *nobody* has ever really caught as he did in most of the Beethoven things. And this is especially true in the early works, where he does something that I suppose was very revolutionary for the time, and something that's in contradiction to everything I've just argued for, because I don't do it at all. I'm very *aware* of constant pulse — Schnabel was aware of the pulse of the *paragraph*. He was certainly aware of the interior pulse as well, but he chose to let it ride through the paragraph, as if he were dictating a letter with a certain series of commas and semicolons, and I don't think anyone else ever played the piano using *that* system successfully — other people have tried, but nobody else ever really got it.

I'm thinking of one gorgeous record, Opus 2, no. 2, in which you really are not aware of the bar line, and in which the structure of the piece could not be more plastic — it's *utterly* clear — but there's no sense of the sort of vertical tension that I, for example, would automatically try to bring to the piece. I would play with very firm, very tight rhythmic features. But Schnabel doesn't. He makes you feel that you're floating through an entire paragraph, and that when you get to the end of that paragraph, no momentum has been lost. Sometimes in the later works I'm not so convinced by some of the things he does; but in those early pieces, as far as I'm concerned, Schnabel could play fast, slow, or in between — it wouldn't make any difference.

And I would like to think that, similarly, I could . . . well, as a matter of fact, perversely enough, my two recorded versions of the Mozart C-Major Sonata, K. 330 employ two very different tempi — one is very slow (the one done in 1958), and the other is of course very fast.

Yes, I agree with you about tempo, I've never understood why it's such a big deal, you know. It's always seemed to me that tempo is a function of so many relatively extraneous things. For instance, my tempi have noticeably slowed down in te last year, because I'm playing on a piano newly rebuilt, which eventually will assume the characteristics that it had before, I hope and pray, but which at the moment has a heavier action. And one by-product of that heaviness is a certain quality of legato which I would frankly like to get rid of — I'd like to get it right back to its nice secco quality that it had before it fell off a truck. But a new piano with new hammers hitting new strings is going to give you *innately* more legato. Now, you can go one of two ways. You can fight it, which I've tried to do to some degree. We have a new record coming out of Bach's first four French Suites [Gould later released an album consisting of the fifth and sixth Suites and Bach's Overture in the French Style] — in fact it's the first thing we did make after the piano was restored — and they're just as deliberate and dry as any Bach I've ever done. But they are played more slowly, because one way you can function within a somewhat thicker sound is obviously to slow down. The articulation, if you adopt the tempo that you might otherwise have done, *is* going to be less clean. So the instrument determines it, as does the hall to an extraordinary extent.

Do you consciously, in your own performances, try to comment on other musicians' interpretations — for instance, playing a Bach work intentionally different from the way Landowska or Edwin Fischer do it?

No, I can honestly tell you that . . . well, I knew many of the Landowska recordings when I was a kid, but I don't believe I've heard any of them since I was about fifteen, and Edwin Fischer I never knew at all. Rather than the playing of people like that, I was much more familiar when I was growing up with the recordings of Rosalyn Tureck, for instance, than I ever was with Landowska. In fact, really I didn't like Landowska's playing very much, and I did like Tureck's enormously — Tureck influenced me.

That's strange. I've found that some of her performances are a bit stiff and artificially terraced.

Well, I think that she and I have very different notions about the music, perhaps. I think that what you've just said about the *strata,* the emphatic terracing in her playing, is partly true. But back in the forties, when I was a teenager, she was the first person who played Bach in what seemed to me a sensible way. In those days, being fourteen, fifteen, sixteen, I was fighting a battle in which I was never going to get a surrender flag from my teacher on the way in which Bach should go, but her records were the first evidence that one did not fight alone. It was playing of such uprightness, to put it into the moral sphere. There was such a sense of a repose that had nothing to do with languor, but rather with moral rectitude in the liturgical sense. Whereas the Bach "specialists," the people who had really brought him to the attention of the many — Casals, Landowska, and so on — played with enormous amounts of rubato. In fact, their whole approach is based on the way in which the Romantic sensibility could be welded onto the baroque, and I think that's really what made their playing very attractive to that generation. Not that it wasn't great playing — it was fantastic playing; perhaps, as playing, better than the people we've been talking about — but nevertheless it, to me, was not really Bach.

Casals has a moment in a documentary I've been working on — it's a line that he always uses, and he used it again with me — in which he talks about the fact that his playing of the Bach Suites for unaccompanied cello was only regarded as revolutionary because, as he put it, the Germans didn't understand him and didn't understand Bach — they didn't understand that Bach was a human being. But I don't agree with him, because — well, I don't know how you feel, but to me the most interesting Bach orchestral performances that I know of on records have come out of Germany — notably Karl Richter's.

But to me, Tureck was a revelation in terms of the way in which Bach could be adapted to the piano. I would think the original recordings that Munchinger made of the *Brandenburgs* must have had much the same revelatory impact. I'm sure this was true for most people of my generation who, shortly after the war, were coming out of a conservatory system which put a premium on expressivity, wanted or not. There was, we were told, something cultivated and cultured about producing a *langueur*, though there were limits of permissibility. For instance, in playing Chopin — which I was never deemed to be able to do, though I had great fun a couple of years ago when I played the B-Minor Sonata on CBC, the only professional Chopinizing of my career — I was always chastened for forgetting about such things as the de-emphasis of the top note in an upward-bound progression. You were supposed to super Bellini's conventions on Chopin's thematic ideas. There were certain expressive conventions of the sort that were supposed to be taken into account, and it wasn't considered good taste to turn these conventions on their head. Above all, it was important that one find some sort of 1945 *Zeitgeist*, and apply it to everything. To play Bach with no pedal at all was just not done. And the models for the teachers of that generation certainly were Casals and Landowska and Fischer. None of those people influenced me in the least; and the one who really did was Tureck.

The composer and pianist Busoni once wrote: "All composers have drawn nearest the true nature of music in preparatory and intermediary passages (preludes and transitions), where they felt at liberty to disregard symmetrical proportions and unconsciously draw free breath." And as examples of what Busoni called the "boundlessness of this pan art," he cited the transition to the last movement of Schumann's D-Minor symphony and the introduction of the fugue of Beethoven's Hammerklavier *Sonata. I wanted to apply this fascinating idea to what seems to be your interest in transitional,* fin-de-siècle *composers like Orlando Gibbons, Max Reger, and Richard Strauss.*

Well, I think you've put your finger on something that I had never really thought about very much — but you're absolutely right — and that is that the repertoire that I'm fondest of tends to emerge from the pens of *fin-de-siècle* men. I can't think of anybody who represents the end of an era better than Orlando Gibbons does, and Gibbons *is* my favorite composer — always has been. I mean, I can't make a case for him being a better contrapuntist than Bach — obviously he wasn't, and obviously he wasn't as gifted a word-colorist as Wagner. There is, however, a spiritual attachment that I began to feel for his music when I was about fourteen or fifteen and first heard some of the anthems; I fell in love with them, and consequently all my life I've wanted to make a Gibbons album of some kind. Unfortunately, there are very few keyboard pieces of quality — his best work is for the voice and not the keyboard — whereas the William Byrd stuff . . . well, I said in my notes on that album that Byrd relates to Gibbons as Strauss to Mahler, and I think the parallel is a valid one. Byrd is both an extrovert and a nostalgist, and that combination is not just effective — it's absolutely irresistible.

But to get back to your point about *fin-de-siècle* composers: It occurs to me that there might be a parallel with my enthusiasm, or lack of it, for nineteenth-century repertoire. I am, as you know, absolutely hooked on all the late-Romantics, or at any rate all of those in the post-Wagnerian tradition — Strauss, Schoenberg in his first style, et cetera — but I do find it very difficult to muster any enthusiasm for the early Romantics. Schumann, for example, is a composer with whom I have very little patience, though Mendelssohn, on the other hand, especially when he's not writing for the piano, appeals to me enormously.

But then, Mendelssohn was probably the most disciplined and classically oriented of the early Romantics.

Exactly.

On the other hand, you play the late Brahms Intermezzi *so beautifully.*

Well, I'm fond of many of them; in fact, I really have great affection for some of them. But I have to be very frank and say that when I sit down and play late-nineteenth-century things for my own amusement, Brahms doesn't often figure in the picture. I'm much more likely to play a Strauss tone poem in my own transcription, or something of the sort. . . . By the way, did I tell you I'm doing my own transcription of *Meistersinger* this weekend?

You're kidding! How many records is that going to take?

Oh, no, not the whole opera [laughing], just the Prelude. You know, I've always sort of sat down at night and played Wagner for myself, because I'm a total Wagnerite — hopelessly addicted to the later things especially — and I thought it would be fun to make my own transcriptions. But I tried to avoid what Liszt does, which is to be very faithful to the original. I preferred to go, if not all the way, then a long way toward a realization rather than a transcription. Anyway, the album will consist of the *Meistersinger* Prelude, which will probably open it, followed by *Dawn* and *Siegfried's Rhine Journey*, and on the flip side the most Germanic (and for "Germanic" read "slowest") performance of *Siegfried Idyll* since — God, what's the name of that man? Knappertsbusch — and which absolutely fits the piano . . . well, can be made to fit the piano, rather as if it had been thought up by Scriabin in his earliest years.

The piece is inherently pianistic — I always thought it would be. I wondered at first about the advisability of a piece that had so much repetition, that was so given to sequences of [sings] four bars of that, and then [sings again] four bars of that, but I found that it could be done by changing the emphasis, the accents on one voice or another. And, in the process, I've developed a thesis about transcription. The whole area is one that really irritated me before, because as a kid everybody was playing the Bach-Liszts or Bach-Tausigs or Bach-Busonis or Bach-something-or-others, and I never did, I didn't like them. I played those things on the organ, and they sounded much better that way.

The Liszt transcriptions, on the other hand, whether of Beethoven or Wagner, tend to be relentlessly faithful, in that if the orchestral texture is thick, Liszt will reproduce that thickness on the piano, and of course a thickness on the piano doesn't sound good, let's face it. If the drum roll goes on for sixteen bars, there will be a tremolando of sixteen bars in the lower octaves of the keyboard, which is impossible pianistically. Now, there are certain places where the timpani have a theatrical role, as in the beginning of the *Rhine Journey*, and where you just can't avoid it. But apart from such moments I took a solemn oath that there wouldn't be anything other than the occasional punctuation from the timpani and that I would try to re-create the pieces as though somebody like Scriabin, who really knew something about the piano, as Wagner did not, had had a hand in it.

The *Meistersinger* is not a problem because it's so contrapuntal that it plays itself, although I must say it's the only place where I'm going to have to cheat, because I'm going to have to put on earphones for the last three minutes, when he brings back all the themes which, if you want to represent them properly, need three hands at least, and preferably four. I've played it as a party piece all my life, and you can usually get through the first seven minutes without incident, and then you say, "Okay, which themes are we leaving out tonight?" So I will do it as an overdub. I've already played the *Siegfried Idyll* on the CBC as a kind of tryout, so I know that *it* works, and what I did therewas horizontalize the sound through arpeggiated chords and similar devices. I took the position that one of the things that goes wrong when you transcribe a work faithfully, especially a work that has a predominant string texture, as the *Siegfried Idyll* does, is that the doubling of contrabass and cello should be either an intermittent feature or one which is used to widen the spectrum of the sound, as indeed it does in the orchestra, without adding to the percussiveness of the sound. So what I did, except in the biggest climaxes, throughout the entire *Siegfried Idyll*, was to have the contrabass always enter on the off beat, much as the timpani in Sibelius's symphonies tend to come in more often than not just before or just after the beat. And that was the prototype for several other little inventions along the way. For example, Wagner frequently sits for six bars or more on an E-major chord, and there's simply no way you can do that on the piano without losing all sense of momentum. Now, Liszt usually falls back on a tremolando, which is just so turn-of-the-century I can't stand it. So what I did — and if you think my Mozart sonatas upset people, wait till the Wagnerians get hold of this — what I did was to invent whole other voices that aren't anywhere in the score, except that they are convincingly Wagnerian. For instance, there's a moment quite near the beginning of the *Siegfried Idyll* where an F-sharp major chord is held for four bars, and over it the violin has the figure [sings]. Now, I just sang it at about twice the tempo at which it is normally played, and if you imagine that played twice as slowly on the piano, you'll realize that the lower notes are bound to be inaudible by the end of the phrase. You can reinforce it, you can hit it again, but I chose not to. What I did, rather, was to invent a dialogue between two offstage horns, one in the tenor and one in the alto, that try to mimic each other [sings the two horns], and they go on like this between themselves, and it's gorgeous . . . forgive me for saying so, but it's gorgeous!

[We hung up on this ecstatic note. A week later Glenn Gould called me to continue and finish up the interview.]

A GLENN GOULD
PICTURE ALBUM

LEFT: Gould at eighteen months of age. *(The National Library of Canada)*
ABOVE: The Toronto Conservatory of Music's Silver Medallists, 1944.
Gould is standing in the back row, on the far right.
(The National Library of Canada)

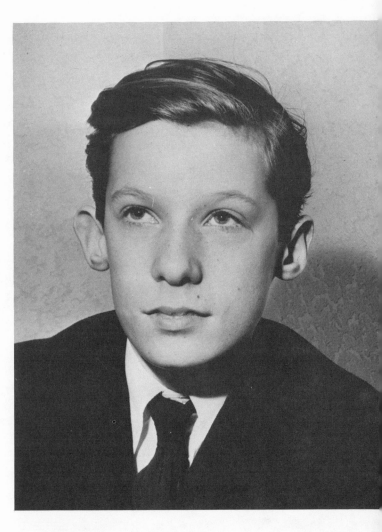

ABOVE: Gould at age fourteen. *(Gordon W. Powley,*
The National Library of Canada) RIGHT: With his pet dog Nicky, 1949.
(The National Library of Canada)

LEFT: Gould in his late teens. *(CBS Records)*
ABOVE: With Vladimir Golschmann, 1958. *(CBS Records)*

Gould in the late sixties. *(CBS Records)*

PART II

*In the intervening period, Gould had gone to the studio
to record the Prelude to Wagner's Die Meistersinger, the
last three contrapuntal minutes of which required him to
overdub another four-handed primo and secundo dialogue.
I asked him how his duets with himself had come out.*

It just went swimmingly, to be immodest about it. At
the end of the *Meistersinger* Prelude, the chap doing the
primo stuff kept indulging in all sorts of strange rubato
conceits, and I had to study his rather eccentric tempo
notions for quite a while until I got with it [laughing], but
once I did, on my secundo part, it was enormous fun. I
had staged the primo fairly cannily — the overdub runs
only about three and a half minutes anyway — so that at
all times the primo consisted of at least two elements —
one that involved something that was continuously in mo-
tion, a sort of perpetuum mobile texture, or at any rate,
whatever figure was fastest. In addition to that, whichever
bass figure was most prominent — not necessarily lowest,
but most prominent — was given to primo, so that I could
hear it over the earphones rather easily.

*Which of the two performers — primo or secundo — did
you prefer?*

Oh, I wouldn't want to play favorites, though the secundo somehow represented all the challenging material,
and the primo, by comparison, all that was rudimentary.
But it really is rather odd, you know, because the moment

you attempt to telegraph an upcoming accelerando or ri-
tard in an overdub, then there's trouble. There's some
little switch that goes "click" inside your head a half-second
before you arrive at that spot, and it's at that fatal moment
that the notion of adjusting a dynamic level or adjusting
a tenuto that will service the telegraphy takes shape. And
if you're charging along in the secundo, to put yourself
into the posture, so to speak, of the primo is no easy task.
In fact, we made them on separate nights, so that I had
to think back twenty-four hours ("Where was I, what was
I thinking about at that moment? When is it going to
happen?"). And those were the troublesome moments, but
they really could be counted on the fingers of one hand;
there weren't more than four or five that were that difficult — it wasn't anything like the marathon I thought it
was going to be.

I wanted to ask you about the extension of this Doppelgänger *syndrome as it appears in your radio and tape
experiments. You've made several little tape-dramas in which
you impersonate a number of "personalities" who seem to
inhabit your mind. And I'm sure that if I were a struc-
turalist, I'd be able to identify at least four of these arche-
typal personages. . . . There is the little tape you made for
Columbia Records to explain how you perform a Bach fugue,
and you introduce three characters who sit around and
confabulate with you. First, there's an elderly, slightly dotty
BBC-type pedagogue named Sir Humphrey. . . .*

[Oxbridge accent] Yes, that's right . . . Price-Davies, I
think.

Then there was some kind of erudite German musicologist.

Well, he usually is, yes . . . I would not have him if he were not entirely skilled . . .

From north or south Germany?

[Herr Gould]: Zat depends entirely upon vether or not you vant him to be civilized or somevat *astringent.* . . . In this case it was a gentleman, as I recall, from south Germany and he spoke with a very *shrill* accent indeed.

Then you have a hippie pianist named Teddy Slotz who plays at the Fillmore and who sounds a bit like a takeoff of Lorin Hollander.

Theodore Slotz, yeah. Everybody kept guessing who this was based on, and you know who it was based on? . . . *Nobody.* Well, no, that's not quite true — there was in my mind a Theodore Slotz, but he was based on a New York taxi driver, whom I met on the occasion of the 1966 off-year elections. I was coming from the Thirtieth Street studio up to my hotel, and the chap who was driving suddenly turned around — I hadn't even thought of it as being election day, it just hadn't occurred to me — and he said, "So, who do you think's going to do pretty good in the election, Mac?" And I said, "Well, I don't know, I guess the governor's got a pretty good chance" — Rockefeller was running for reelection — and he looked at me (*he* had initiated the subject) and said, "Yah don' expect me to talk politics wit yah, do yah, Mac? I mean, like, there're two things I don't never talk about in this

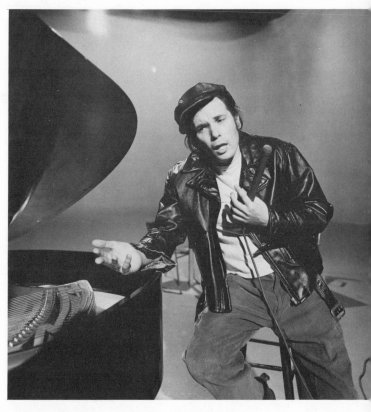

Gould as Theodore Slotz, a fictional character
inspired by a New York City taxi driver Gould once met.
(Robert C. Ragsdale, The National Library of Canada)

cab, one's politics and the other's religion, know what I mean? I never talk about that, man. No offense to you personally, man. I don't know if you're a Democrat or a Republican." "Well, I'm Canadian, so I'm not really either of those things." "Well, I don't care where yah come from, Mac, but yah can't trust people these days, yah know what I mean? Like I'll tell yah a story, Mac, like just last week I had a guy in the cab — he was from Venezuela, yah know — and he says to me, he says, 'What do yah think about Rockefeller?' So I says, 'Aw, that s.o.b.,' yah know. Well, it turns out them Venezuelans are really hot on the Rockefellers. Now, I didn't know that, how's I supposed to know that? This guy got so mad I don't get no tip. 120th Street! 120th Street, man, I don't get no tip." At that moment Theodore Slotz was born.

And from that moment on, whenever I wanted to do an American hippie, that taxi driver came into my mind; but I really didn't have any musical archetype in mind at all.

What's fascinating about all of these routines is the fact that you touch on really interesting ideas — about Bach's evolutionary approach to composition, for example, as you talk about it on that tape. This whole idea of impersonation reminds me of one of your articles in which you talked about Van Meegeren, the famous forger of Vermeer paintings, and suggested that the forger is the hero of electronic culture. I can't help but relate this Doppelgänger *idea to your series of impersonations. There's something of the trickster in all of this, isn't there?*

It's a very interesting tack you're endeavoring to take. I would love to go along with it; I'd have to think about it a bit and maybe call you back in a month and say, "Yes, you're right." I am fascinated with the fact that most of our value judgments relate to an awareness of identity; we tend to be terribly frightened of making judgments if we're not aware of the identity of whoever is responsible for a piece of art. And I am fascinated with that idea — in fact, my most joyous moments in radio, as opposed to my most creative ones, perhaps, are those when I can turn to impersonation. As a matter of fact, Theodore Slotz turns up fairly frequently on my programs as a sort of intermission guest, and he usually has something unkind to say about my performances. On one occasion, he caught a few people off guard, I guess, although the context should have made it quite clear that this was a put-on, but the switchboard lit up with abusive calls — "How dare they let this idiotic young beat critic tear our local talent apart?"

To be serious, though, I'm absolutely convinced, despite the old saw about the fact that a good novelist is someone who does not need a *nom de plume*, that a certain part of your persona operates efficiently within the structure of a certain life style, a certain name, while another part may operate best only providing you change those factors. I, for instance, was incapable of writing in a sustained humorous style until I developed an ability to portray myself pseudonymously. I started this in the mid-sixties. I wrote a few articles for *High Fidelity* in which I turned up a a critic named Herbert von Hochmeister who lived in the Northwest Territories. The reason for that metaphor was that Herbert could thereby survey the culture of North America from his exalted remove, and pontificate accordingly. The character was also vaguely based on Karajan: Von Hochmeister was a retired conductor and was always spouting off about Germanic culture and things of that nature. At least, that's how I got into the character. Once having got into it, I had to make him sufficiently aware of other and more recent innovations so that he could speak of them with some authority. But in any event, once I did that, I found it no problem at all to say what I wanted to say in a humorous style. Until then, there was a degree of inhibition that prevented me from doing so. But then the floodgates were open, and subsequently I developed a character for every season.

I wanted to ask you about your experiments with quad-raphonic sound. I know you tried recording a Bach fugue, playing each of the four musical lines separately and then allocating each to its own speaker.

First of all, the results, in terms of performance per se, were appalling. They weren't expected to be otherwise, because nobody thought that I was going to turn into the First Piano Quartet overnight. It was an in-house demonstration, purely and simply that, and in fact it came up literally at the last minute. We had a couple of hours left over in the session and somebody said, "Will you do this for us," so I did it. But the whole question of quad, it seems to me, is interesting at the moment because it's going through so many sea changes — it's still on its shake-down cruise, really.

Well, take the quad recording of Bartók's Concerto for Orchestra, *which features "surround" sound, so that you hear it as if you were sitting in the middle of the orchestra.*

It's an interesting idea, but this is one of Bartók's more traditional and formally "classical" works, and what this quad approach does is to analyze that piece and then re-fashion it in a sonic and structural perspective which seems to go against its grain — much as it would with a Mozart and Beethoven symphony.

If one thinks in terms of a proscenium stage, as one does for classical music, it certainly does. I've argued this point with my producer, Andy Kazdin, and others at Columbia with some vehemence, because I basically argue from *your* point of view when we're talking about things like Beethoven symphonies, or whatever.

I assumed you automatically preferred "surround" sound. You once gave an interview in which you criticized the ambient coughing-in-the-back type of quad recording . . .

No, I don't, that's not at all true. Because in that case I'd never look at a black-and-white movie. On the contrary, I prefer mono sound for certain kinds of things. I think that there are certain works that don't benefit even by left and right separation. Quadraphony is not necessarily about Bach trio sonatas or Beethoven symphonies at all.

Now, when for Gabrieli they station four brass choirs around the room, then, of course, that's perfectly feasible. There's a piece by a Dutchman, a contemporary of Beethoven's, whose name I can't remember, for four string quartets and orchestra — really anticipatory of Elliott Carter — which is quite an extraordinary piece. Phillips recorded it fairly recently, and I saw the score. That's a natural piece from the classical period for quad. But there aren't many such things, and unless you want to do something very radical with the repertoire — maybe these words will come back to haunt me — I can't really see that the bulk of the classical repertoire is designed for quad.

I think that I've probably moderated my views about rear-end ambience since I gave that interview. I see nothing really wrong with it, as long as it doesn't assault you with the notion that you are back in the concert hall, because after all that's precisely what the recording got you out of. To put you back there and say that *that*'s the ultimate achievement seems to me to defeat the purpose of the recording. But if indeed the added ambience does something to enhance the presence of the acoustical environment overall, that's something else again.

Color can be an enhancement of black-and-white, but it doesn't have to be, and there are lots of things that work much better in black-and-white: I mean, I would not want to see *Woman in the Dunes* in color. Let me take another example: think of *Miss Julie*, for instance. Implicit in the structure of the play, which is a very tight structure, is the notion of light — northern light, as it happens — light that barely goes below the horizon and never altogether loses its power, and which in the end is much stronger than when the play opened. Now, presumably some hotshot director could come along with a new angle on Strindberg and say that *Miss Julie* should really be set in Bolivia. In that case, we'd have sudden blackouts come sundown, and I'm not at all sure that that wouldn't work. But if it worked, you'd have to rethink the characterization, you'd have to restructure the whole relationship of Jean and Julie and Christine so that the matriarchal triangulation reflected a tropical as opposed to a Nordic culture. I think that's as good a parallel as any that I can think of — *that* notion of *that* action taking place on Midsummer Night was not accidental. It was absolutely indigenous to the structure of the play and to the sense of the importance of hesitancy in class interrelationship — that was the whole point of that play, really. Set that in Bolivia, and it isn't going to work — unless you change the characters. That isn't to say it would be a less compelling creation, it's just that it would be a different creation, and I think you have to start from scratch. So, I suppose by the same yardstick you could design an experience around a classical work that would work in quad.

Would you give an example of how you'd go about doing this?

I have in the can an eight-track version of a Scriabin sonata. Now, of course, this was overkill in relation to any pianistic needs, obviously: Four-track would already be overkill, but this was quadruple overkill. It was done, however, with the idea, as yet unrealized because unmixed, that it would be interesting to see what would happen if you opted for the notion that a piano was not a piano was not a piano, that it didn't have to be locked into one acoustic environment from first groove to last. By which I don't mean that it was being pan-potted all over the place.

Pan-potting?

"Pot" in the sense of potentiometer and "pan" as in panning across. . . . Pan-potting is a way of precisely rather than organically — that sounds like a contradiction but

I'll explain what I mean by it in a minute — moving one or more sound sources about a room.

Let me give you an example — this is just a parenthesis, we'll eventually get back to what we're talking about: If, for instance, I have a voice on my tape recorder, such as that of Maestro Casals (with whose voice I've been living for the past few weeks, since I'm making a documentary about him), and if I want to move it across from the left speaker to the right, I can do that in one of two ways. I can start it off full left, gradually open the right channel and move it to a center screen, or, if I simultaneously close the left pot, full right. But if I want to take that source and — in the process of a complicated mix involving, let's say, two or three other characters speaking at the same time perhaps, and music on another couple of tracks — confine it to one track as opposed to two tracks, then the only way in which I can move it is by pan-pot. It's like a swing of the audio camera, but it provides for a degree of precision in terms of repositioning the sound source that would be hard to duplicate via the two-track, left-versus-right movement that I described first.

Anyway, as that voice moves across the room towards center stage, it will appear to have gone up towards the ceiling, rather than to have moved in a straight line. This doesn't, generally speaking, affect orchestral placement, because we've grown inured to the idea that strings are on the left, which seems all wrong to me as a pianist. I mean, everybody knows that high notes are played by something that's on the right, right? [laughing] But this simulated elevation is a disadvantage which one can turn to good account on occasion. For example, in my documentary on Newfoundland, I positioned an elderly minister in such a manner as to suggest a pulpit-like location.

However, this kind of advantage is greatly outweighed by the fact that as you move sound sources about, the nature of that particular vertical triangulation does distort the sense of line that's inherent in the image. Now, in the same way, when, in quad, you listen to sound coming at you from four corners of a room, you're also dealing with the business about who sits where and who gets the best view in the house — in Germany the father would; in America the mother would; and in France, I suppose, the mistress would. You're dealing with multiple triangles and not with the absolute, razor-sharp, pinpoint accuracy that you want for character placement.

I think that a possible solution is to fill out the space with many more speakers, but to use them in order to flatten the surface, to minimize the multiple triangulations we were talking about, which I think constitutes the great drawback of quad at the moment.

I really think that quad has a much greater potential for the spoken word than for music. I mean, if you were going to represent the Shakespearean theater in the round, how else than by quad? That would be magnificent — utterly magnificent. But anyway, I don't think that you can deal with a Haydn string quartet and simply treat it as you would Elliott Carter's — I don't think that's what it's all about. And there I come right back to your corner.

End of parenthesis. Now, what we did with the Scriabin was to record the piece with four different mike perspectives — my conventional perspective, which is for most people's taste too close and too tight and too taut and which is usually about five feet away from the instrument, then a somewhat more discreet, more conventionally European pickup, perhaps eight or nine feet away, again with a rank of three mikes. Those were respectively the second and third ranks. Rank number one was the sort of pickup that you might have used for Art Tatum twenty years ago — the mikes were right inside the piano, almost lying on the strings, ultrapercussive. But, curiously enough, not at all unsatisfying. It had a kind of whiskery quality that was very pleasant — you could feel every note bristling, and that was very nice.

The final perspective, or nonperspective, consisted of two mikes pointing at the far wall — pointing *at* the wall, and not at the piano, so that they were picking up the ambience. And the Scriabin sonata in question, which was the fifth one, starts with a trill in the lowest octave of the piano, supported by a tritonic passage played as a tremolando, and in the course of about ten seconds this trill plus the accompanying tritone moves up the keyboard, octave by octave, until it gets to the very top, at which point the score unrealistically asks for fortissimo, and, of course, you can't play fortissimo at the top of the piano. Anyway, it moves theoretically from pianissimo to fortissimo, and it also moves from octave to octave with the same set of quasi-magic-chord notes. What we did was to record the whole piece with these four perspectives and decide that at some time in the future it would be nice to choreograph it, to look at the score and decide what it might offer in terms of a cinematic projection, what opportunities it might afford for long shots, tight shots, two-shots, dissolves, hard cuts, jump cuts, whatever. If you thought of it in those terms, how would you design this piece for sound cameras?

Well, we managed to excite some very blasé engineers by experimenting with the place I've just described—starting off with the hindmost mikes, those that faced the wall, and which picked up sort of a distant rumble, which was really quite an unearthly sound. I'm just trying to equate it with what listeners might think when they first heard it — for one second it would sound God-awful, and they'd think, "What is that?" Anyway, with each octave, as it moved up the piano, we'd kick in another rank of mikes, but never so many that the sound lost its basic clarity. For instance, as rank two came in, four went out, so we then had two and three combined. As one came in, three went out, and so on. We finally ended up on the topmost notes, those that Scriabin specified as fortissimo, but which can't be played fortissimo, with the Art Tatum pickup (or the Oscar Peterson pickup or whatever you want to call it).

Like a zoom.

Right, it was a zoom, it was a ten-second zoom right to that *thing*, and it was one of the most dazzling audio effects I've ever heard. At that point in the score there's a pause — a fermata — then an eighth-note rest, and then Scriabin starts his main theme, if you can call it that, at which point we pull back to perspective two, our conventional pickup, and the movement proper begins. Now, that kind of thing, if you extend its implications to quad, could, I think, produce some really interesting results.

You could also theoretically move that sequence around the room topologically from one corner to the other. That would be another kind of "shot."

Absolutely. But I think, again, that if you did that, you might prefer to have recorded it in a different way. I mean, we recorded it with the idea in mind that we were locked into left-right stereo, even though quad was a known quantity at the time: Now, what would that difference be? I don't really know. Perhaps it wouldn't be so much a question of recording it differently as of presenting it differently. [The above techniques are embodied in Gould's November 1977 release of Sibelius's *Three Sonatines*, Opus 67, and *Kyllikki*, Opus 41.]

There's a moment in the radio documentary I made about Stokowski which is, I think, quite magical. It's a moment, prior to which, for some ten minutes, Stokowski had been talking about his experience with recording in the early days of his association with the Philadelphia Orchestra, beginning in 1917. He talked about making records in the twenties and his experiments at the Bell Lab and the fact that they built a research studio for him under the stage at the Academy of Music in Philadelphia. During this sequence the only possible illustration I could think of was Stokowski's own 78rpm catalog, and we managed to use a number of brief excerpts from his recordings of that era, employing a deliberately primitive, monaural style of stereo. Obviously we *were* in stereo, we couldn't deny that, but I took these 78s and fed them alternately to left and right speakers at a fairly snappy pace, and with each example succeeding the preceding one by three or four

Gould with Leopold Stokowski, 1966. *(CBS Records)*

years, so that within a space of seven or eight minutes we moved from about 1917, with the *Rienzi* Overture, to about 1934, with his first recording of Wagner's "Good Friday Spell." And in so doing, I used nothing but hard cuts, whereas my natural inclination in treating Stokowski to a sound portrait was to use dissolves, because he's a dissolve man and not a hard-cut man — he cries out for a Visconti and not a Bergman.

Anyway, at the end of the sequence I faced a real problem, because somehow I had to get him back to time present, if only because he was about to say something elegiac — I can't remember the exact line, but I think it was "Today it is much better than in the past, but I believe we can do better still" — in that delightful tone of his. And so I had to find a way of suggesting this betterment, and at the same time bringing us back into the present, because by this time we were forty minutes into the show and we'd spent thirty of those minutes with contemporary stereo sound. And I discovered that he had remade the "Good Friday Spell" in 1960.

And just on a wild chance I got out the record, timed various segments — his views about the work hadn't changed to any great extent at all over the years — and found one segment, of no less than twenty-five seconds, which ran within three quarters of a second of the 1934 version. So what we managed to do was to have the 1934 version going to the left speaker — I used probably fifteen or sixteen seconds of it solo — and then, also in the left, began to super, note by note, the 1960 version, to which we applied a good deal of compression so that the frequency response would not at first sound appreciably different from the earlier recording. Then, gradually, we opened the right channel and moved the stereo version across the screen. The 1934 version suddenly appeared to move, to grow, to creep out of the left wall, to become almost incandescent. But the effect was that during the phrase "Things are better than they were," the sound was not yet so good that you wanted to say, "Whoopee." On the contrary, you wanted to say with him, "Yeah, it could be better than that . . . but how the hell do they do that!" It's a moment I'm very proud of.

Many people don't know much about the several radio documentaries you've made for the Canadian Broadcasting Corporation. You've spoken about your dissatisfaction with the linear quality of radio — the over-to-you-and-now-back-to-your-host wrap-up approach. Two of your programs — The Idea of North *and* The Latecomers — *are both about the idea of solitude as it affects people living in northern Canada and Newfoundland. And in these programs you used all sorts of contrapuntal effects — trio sonata, fugal counterpoint, and basso ostinato forms — in structuring and displaying the voices of the persons heard on the programs. Now, you've also talked about the idea of the media in relationship to sensory deprivation. How does this idea relate to your ideas about radio?*

That's a huge question, so let me try to tackle it one point at a time. The first point that you mentioned was the fact that both those programs deal to some degree with solitude. In fact, so do all of the major documentaries I've made. There are six programs thus far that have taken three or four hundred hours of studio time each. Number one was, as you mentioned, *The Idea of North*, two was *The Latecomers*, three was *Stokowski*, four is the one that we're just mixing now about Casals (*Casals: A Portrait for Radio*). Five, a fantasy-documentary on Schoenberg which is intended for his centennial next year (*Schoenberg: The First 100 Years*). And there's one other program which has lain around now for a year and a half, it's been ready for mixing for a year and a half and hasn't been yet. It's a program on the Mennonites which is called *The Quiet in the Land — Die Stillen in dem Lande* is what they call themselves — and that is the ultimate in community isolation. So next I want to do a comedy about an isolated man, because I'm sick and tired of these profound statements [laughing].

To some extent or other, all of the subjects that I've chosen have had to do with isolation — even the musical ones. I mean, certainly Stokowski is not exactly a mainstream figure; he's a man who has deliberately decided to go his own way, as has Casals, for other reasons. In any event, all six programs have had to do in some way with isolation, and most particularly, of course, the three that have been about groups of individuals. Because the first group were people who had for one reason or another chosen to isolate themselves in the north — all of them at this stage in their lives are out of it. But precisely because of the success of that program, one person has changed his life: programs, you know, have a funny way of changing people's lives, as the *American Family* is only too well aware. But in any event, that program put together a group of individuals and compared their individual experiences.

The Latecomers dealt with a subject for which I didn't

In commemoration of Canada's Centennial in 1967, *The Toronto Sun* published a feature on distinguished citizens. Left to right: Morley Callaghan, Sir Ernest MacMillan, Kate Reid, A.Y. Jackson, Glenn Gould, and Marshall McLuhan. (THE TORONTO SUN, *The National Library of Canada*)

feel the same sense of sympathy at all, because the whole idea of the herd gathering — no matter how splendid and remote the rock on which they isolate themselves — doesn't really appeal to me. The subject of the program was nominally the viability of outport life. Outports are simply villages devoid of conveniences, and geographically isolated from the outside world — villages not serviced by a main highway or something of the sort.

The village we talked about — though it wasn't where most of the people involved came from, I just pretended that they all came from there — was a village called St. Joseph's, which is a ghost town now, and our chief spokesman, our narrator, who is at present the dean of the faculty of arts at the university down there, had come from this village. A few months before I made the program, he had been back to see the community pulling up stakes, quite literally, and he had to escort his father, who had been the last of the village to leave. It was a very touching story as he told it, and it made sense to me to unify the program and suggest that all these disparate characters were in some way involved with that village. And in order to do that I then had to sketch imaginary family relationships and to create quasidramatic exchanges between the main characters, which would lend credence to those relationships.

Marshall McLuhan once wrote that radio is a "hot" medium, television a "cool" one. I've always felt the opposite. Radio always seems to allow you to turn inward — into your own solitude — and to contact your fantasies, whereas television just zonks you out and doesn't really let you participate in much of anything.

I agree, and I think that he made that distinction not so much in deference to what he thought or didn't think about radio — I have the sneaking suspicion that Marshall doesn't listen to that much radio, frankly — but that he was *aiming it*, structuring it, so that he could eventually distinguish between film and television, which was never a distinction that convinced me either.

I admire McLuhan very much — at one time he was a neighbor, as a matter of fact, but he's moved since — and I still see him once in a while; he's a dear and wonderful man. But I always felt that he would have been better off without that sort of trendy terminology that he got off on in *Understanding Media*, and that we would have understood him better without it. I never did really try to figure out what it meant, though I remember arguing endlessly with him one time, which is an exercise in futility in itself: You do not argue with Marshall, you wait for a *probe*; there's no guarantee that his answer will relate in any helpful way to your question. The answers will be illuminating and exciting and animating, but they will not necessarily be in response to your questions. So there's no possibility of an argument. But in any event, I tried to suggest to him that at a time when the medium of television was gobbling up films at a great rate and putting them out at all hours of the day — not just for the late, late viewer, as had been the case maybe two decades ago — that it was futile to try and make that distinction.

Take the idea of radio as a metaphor for solitude. It's a much more private experience. Why do you think you're so interested in this inward-turning medium?

I'd like to deal with this as sensibly as I can, because it's a big question, it's an important question. I don't know what the effective ratio would be, but I've always had some sort of intuition that for every hour that you spend in the company of other human beings you need X number of hours alone. Now, what that X represents I don't really know; it might be two and seven-eighths or seven and two-eighths, but it's a substantial ratio. Radio, in any case, is a medium I've been very close to ever since I was a child, that I listen to virtually nonstop: I mean, it's wallpaper for me — I sleep with the radio on, in fact now I'm incapable of sleeping *without* the radio on, ever since I gave up Nembutal [laughing].

Does it affect your dreams?

Sure, in the sense that if there are newscasts on the hour, I pick up the bulletins and use them as the subjects for my dreams. In the morning, if there's been a boat that's just gone down, I'll think, "Gee, that was an odd dream about the *Titanic* I had last night," and then pick up the paper at the door: *"Lusitania* Sinks," and I will, of course, have concocted my own dream variation on the story already.

I've never conceded any real contradiction between the assumption that one can have a rather solitary existence and the fact that one can supportively have radio in the background at all times. I mean, we talked last week about a purely physical demonstration of its power — you know, its power to block out mental impediments; we talked about Beethoven's Opus 109. I'm totally incapable of understanding people who get upset with any kind of Muzak. I can go up and down on endless elevators and never be bothered by it. No matter how insipid the stuff may be, I really don't care — I'm utterly undiscriminating.

Maybe your feelings about solitude come from the fact that you've got a Nordic temperament.

That certainly is part of it. It's an ambition of mine, which I never seem to get around to realizing, to spend at least one winter north of the Arctic Circle. Anyone can go there in the summer when the sun is up, but I want to go there when the sun is down, I really do, and so help me I'm going to do it one of these times. I've said this now for five or six years, and every year the schedule gets in the way.

What would you do about playing the piano up there?

I don't need to play it. But I'm sure the local bar has got a piano I could noodle on if necessary. Well, to be truthful, once a month or so I've literally got to touch the piano or I stop sleeping properly. That really is true. I was in Newfoundland last summer, just as a tourist, and after about a month I found that I was getting by on three and four hours a night, which seemed ridiculous, because I was doing reasonably energetic things like wandering up and down cliffs and beaches and cuing the surf for all sorts of imaginary documentaries . . . and this was insane, because I was getting more and more tired every day. And finally I realized that what was missing was the fact that I *did* need contact with a piano just for an hour or so. And, literally, that will do me for a month; that's all that's necessary. As it happened I knew of a delightful old German

Steinway located at the CBC studios in St. John's, which I discovered when I was down there doing *The Latecomers* four years before; I asked if I could have an hour with it, which they granted, and the next night, you know—sound as a baby.

I really get a feeling of autumn from your performances — with that special clear and measureless light.

Good. Then my life has not been in vain [laughing]. . . . You know, back in my touring days, whenever I had to head into the American South or into the European South — I never have been below the equator so I can't talk about the South American experience at all — I was profoundly depressed, and not just because of the papier-mâché quality of places like Miami Beach or most of Los Angeles. It really had something to do with the quality of the light, with the sudden fadeouts at night, for example. I got very depressed, and that depression usually rubbed off on my playing. Whereas, on the contrary, the best month of my life — in many ways the most important precisely because it was the most solitary — was spent in Hamburg, where I was ill . . . though I must admit in rather luxurious surroundings, I'd managed to get myself booked into a hotel called the Vier Jahreszeiten, which translates as the Four Seasons and which looks out on one of the most splendid views of Hamburg, which city at that time was in the process of rebuilding.

And I had come down with something called focal nephritis, which is a mild variant of a very dangerous kidney disease, but in this case just viral-induced and something that takes about a month to cure. Anyway, I had to stay, in a semiquarantined state, in the Vier Jahreszeiten, and knowing nobody in Hamburg turned out to be the greatest blessing in the world. I guess this was my Hans Castorp period; it was really marvelous.

There is a sense of exaltation — I'm careful about using that word, but it's the only word that really applies to that particular kind of aloneness. It's an experience that most people don't permit themselves to know. I'm convinced of that; certainly, from time to time, most of us, because of the pressures of work or whatever, lose contact with it. But there has to be a way of redressing that balance and reestablishing that ratio that I talked about earlier. And sooner or later I'm going to spend a winter in the dark; I'm convinced of that, too.

You once wrote an article about Petula Clark which appeared in High Fidelity *magazine, and in it you compared her favorably with the Beatles. In fact, you even put the Beatles down. And I seem to remember that you identified Petula Clark with yourself in some way.*

Well, [laughing], there was a little leg-pulling in that article. However, I *would* compare her favorably with the Beatles, that wouldn't take much doing.

How do you explain such a sacrilege?

Well, first of all let me tell you about the article itself and then about the sacrilege. That article was something I put more work into than anything of its length I've ever written before — in fact, I think six months separated its last word from its first. It had a very interesting formal plan — it was a sort of *Spiegelbild*, as the Germans would say; it was a mirror image. As a matter of fact, if you want a musical parallel, think of the Webern *Variations for Piano*, first movement.

You mean that your Petula Clark essay was a kind of homage to Anton Webern?

Well, it had more thirty-second notes, so to speak, and a much denser texture than Webern would allow. But reduced to its skeleton, as you might say, there is a structural relationship between my article on Petula and Webern's Opus 27. And after all, if Thomas Mann could be persuaded to write *Tonio Kröger* through the study of Haydn's sonata-allegros — why not?

The mirror was inserted in the middle of the third scene — there were five scenes in the piece. Numbers one and five were set along Highway 17 in northern Ontario and dealt with a drive I took to and away from the town of Marathon; Petula isn't even mentioned until the closing lines of scene one. Scenes two, three, and four, however, deal directly *with* her — two with the first Tony Hatch songs ("Downtown" and "My Love") which made her famous; there were many songs that Tony "hatched" (bad pun) for her, but those were her big hits of the early sixties. Scene four, on the other hand, deals primarily with "Who Am I?" which came along a couple of years later. But the climax of the scenes that deal with Petula — the mirror—was inserted in the center of scene three, and dealt with the comparison that you referred to between Petula and the Beatles.

And then, I suppose, all the images went into retrograde inversion, or something like that?

Something *very* like that. I should add, though, that the highway trip was not exclusively metaphorical. I actually did become aware of her early hits while driving that road — *that* much was true; it didn't actually take place in Marathon as I suggested, but I used that town because I know it rather well and because it led me to an irresistible bit of symbolism.

Marathon is the sort of town that would have delighted Franz Kafka — I think I described that at great length in the piece — because the bureaucratic structure and stratification of the town is emphasized by the kind of houses you find on various streets as you ascend from the harbor. In any event, I really did discover Petula on the highway, and not too many miles from where I said it happened.

But you did discover her on the radio.

Oh, yes, sure, sure — I'd never bought a pop record in my life. But after that I picked up every record she'd ever made. . . . We're getting now to the point where I leave the metaphor aside — no, no, let me say one more thing about that. The upbeat songs that I dealt with in scene two — "Downtown" and "My Love" — were related to the fact that, in Marathon, when you drive up the banks of the fjord on which the town is set, beyond the last and most distinguished row of houses, you reach a gate leading to the lumber run at the top of Marathon Point, with a sign saying PROCEED NO FURTHER. And, at this point, my article on Petula had reached "My Love" and "Downtown," both of which were songs of outgoingness; they were songs of burgeoning maturity, supposedly. Subsequently, I remember discovering with great delight, with an almost Milton Babbitt-ish delight, that "Who Am I?" employed the inverse motive of "Downtown." It was a song of total despair, and became, of course, the prime topic of scene four. Anyway, the downcast songs, the songs of disillusionment, of maturity by-passed — like "Who Am I?" — contrasted with my setting off from Marathon in search of another kind of town that was laid out in a different kind of way. And that was the metaphor I was trying to pursue.

Why did you criticize the Beatles?

I have to say that I was appalled then, as I am now, by what the Beatles did to pop music. I recall that Ned Rorem once said that they were the best tune-writers since Schubert, or something of the sort. It was very *au courant* to say that kind of thing at the time I wrote my article, and I really was so outraged by this point of view, which I could not and cannot understand, that I felt somebody had to debate this Rorem-esque theory, however indirectly.

You know, there's a marvelous description of Mussorgsky in some biography or other in which he gets very drunk one night at a musicale, which was by no means unusual behavior for him, and takes off at Mendelssohn, who of course was several decades dead at that point. Mendelssohn, according to Mussorgsky, had ruined European music in the nineteenth century. And, to Mussorgsky's mind, that which Mendelssohn had sinned against was the sense of fantasy. I'm paraphrasing like mad, of course, that was not the exact quote, it was much more colorful than that. But the whole sort of deeply-into-your-cups, fantasy-struck madness that the Romantic movement spawned in the nineteenth century, and particularly with isolated types like Mussorgsky — isolated from the Central Western European tradition — was opposed to what Mendelssohn stood for. And that is very odd when you think of it, because Mussorgsky's successors were people like Shostakovich, who, for one reason or another, have been compelled to take note of Marxist doctrine, which holds that art is there to purify the masses, and of course there cannot be a more purifying, i.e., read, *law-abiding*, experience than the Mendelssohnian structure. But this, of course, was precisely what Mussorgsky objected to. And the point of my Shostakovich comparison is that the Russians obviously have had to confront, somehow incorporate, and yet at the same time demythologize, the Mendelssohnian legacy. But in any event, Mussorgsky didn't understand Mendelssohn, and I suspect for much the same reason that the Beatles would find it hard to understand Petula Clark.

I disagree with you about your musical criticism, but what about the Beatles' lyrics, which seem to me really special?

Well, of course, I was appalled by two aspects — one relates purely to the music, but the other involves the general production level that was encouraged by the Beatles at that time, though, to be fair, not spawned by them. There was, as you know, a tendency throughout all of the pop business in the sixties, particularly in areas that involved rock — acid or otherwise — to keep *that* pot or *those* pots which controlled the conveyers of the word, *down* — down, that is, in relation to the instrumental tracks, which were always *up*.

Now, I think that this tendency is much less prevalent today, but to those of us who grew up with the notion that pop music had something to do with big band sound — and at the risk of dating myself, that's my period — this is an appalling notion; indeed, I would have to say abstractly that it's an appalling recording notion at any time. Certainly, there's no particular reason why a certain effect should not be enhanced by lowering the primary track. But to *always* have it down, to make everybody grope for the lyrics, seems to me very foolish. I think, perhaps, I *do* understand the psychological reason, but I don't agree with it.

In any event, having said that, I have to tell you that avoiding the Beatles as best I could in the sixties — which was no mean feat — I really don't know the lyrics, I know a few fragments from them, I know the titles, but I couldn't recite more than half a dozen lines in all. So I really was speaking primarily on the musical level. The lyrics that do come through with the pot up tend to be the late ones and the early ones — the ones in between that made them a cause célèbre, do not — at least not to my ear. I mean, "I Want to Hold Your Hand" — you can understand that; "Let It Be" — you can understand that. And almost everything in between is sort of way down there, buried under piles of garbage, of instrumental garbage.

So I really can talk with some authority only about the music, and, as I've said, I find it appalling. You see, I think Mussorgsky was accurate in his observation and wrong in his concept: I think his observation that Mendelssohn was a strait-laced man who liked nice, tidy sixteen-bar paragraphs was quite correct. What he forgot to notice was that Mendelssohn was inventive on another level altogether. In order to comprehend his invention, one has to first accept that *placidity* that is the most abundant feature of his music. Having accepted that, Mendelssohn can then surprise you by the gentlest movement; he needs only the tiniest change, as they say in the jazz field, to make his effect felt. Whereas in the case of Mussorgsky, he has to hit you over the head with a forte-piano contrast, or a quasi-modal moment or something — I happen to like Mussorgsky, by the way, I really do. He wasn't very competent technically, of course, but then neither were the Beatles. However, I think that the point was indicative of a misunderstanding — and this wouldn't apply just to composers — that has always muddied the waters for artists who assume that invention has something to do with the noise you make while breaking rules. Needless to say, I don't think it does. I think it has to do with the subtlety with which you adhere to premises somewhat different from those that may be expected of you. I cannot bear assaults of any kind, and it seems to me that the Beatles essentially were out to affront and to assault.

It's strange that a lot of your recordings have the kind of effect on certain persons that you say the Beatles' recordings have on you.

[Laughing] Well, I cannot top that, sir, and I don't think I should even try. In my view, my recordings have the same effect that Petula Clark's should have had, but why don't we leave that judgment to posterity.

But, you know, about ten years ago, I used to hear some very well-meaning people say that they tended to listen to classical music only when it had a beat, as it did in my playing, because they were jazz-oriented. Now, I could at least identify with that comment to some degree. I wasn't interested in the jazz scene either, but in my teens, I went through a period when it was very "in" to see profundities in Lennie Tristano, and I tried, so help me, I tried, but I never succeeded.

I was once playing a friend a recording of Renaissance music performed by England's Musica Reservata, a wonderful group which emphasizes close-miked sound, clear textures, rhythmic precision, vibratoless voices, and a soprano who sings with a nasal quality similar in timbre and force to that of certain gypsy vocalists. And this friend said: "This group's the Glenn Gould of Renaissance music!"

Well, that really is very flattering, but it occurs to me that the kind of clarity that you're talking about is not, never could be, the exclusive preserve of one individual or orchestra or group or chorus: it relates to a state of mind, obviously. In fact, I even wonder whether it relates exclusively, or primarily, to music which involves a continuo-like rhythmic pulse. I would think, just to play the devil's advocate for a moment, that if the music can be conducted — mentally, that is, and always assuming a ready supply of subdivided beats on behalf of the listener — the battle is already half-won.

I would have to argue, for example, that, at her best, and given her best material, Barbra Streisand, whose fan I happen to be, is probably the greatest singing-actress since Maria Callas — and I hyphenate very carefully, in the sense of "singing-actress." For instance, if you take a rubato-filled song like "He Touched Me" — at least it's full of rubato in Streisand's rendition, and it's a magnificent structure harmonically, by the way; I mean, it's as good as anything Fauré ever wrote, it really is — you find that the sense of tempo change, the sense of key change, is all part of one structural concept, which of course reveals a sense of unity that plays no part at all in what is to my mind the ultrasimplistic notions that the Beatles were trying to pass off.

See, I think what I was trying to say about the Beatles was that after all of the pretension has been cut away and after all the faddish admiration of the Cathy Berberians of this world has been removed, what you really have left is three chords. Now, if what you want is an extended exercise in how to mangle three chords, then obviously the Beatles are for you; but, on the other hand, if you prefer to have the same three chords unmangled — just played nicely — then Tony Hatch is your man.

At the same time, I do think that what I said before about the Mendelssohn-Mussorgsky polarity is absolutely valid, that there happens to be a "quirk quotient" in the former's work which is minimal, but which is noticeable precisely because it *is* minimal. In Mussorgsky, in Janáček — let's take another example of the same strain — in Berlioz, the quirk quotient is very great, which is to say that the unexpected happens very frequently, and consequently it takes a tremendous gesture in order to really surprise you. In Mendelssohn it doesn't — just the tiniest movement, just one hair not *quite* in place.

Now it is my thesis, which at this point has to be subdivided, that (a) the Beatles themselves, those who wrote, and they're notably Lennon and McCartney, and (b) those who advised them in the production sense, the studio, did not have that kind of control, didn't really know where they were going. They seemed to want to say, "We are going to show you that it is possible to work with a minimal harmonic structure and to so becloud the issue that that's what we're doing that you're going to think it's new and it's different and whoopee!" And all of this eclectic garbage — I mean, you don't necessarily get it good by adding a sitar, that's really the point, I think.

But in classical Chinese music, for example, the pitch interest is minimal, and things like articulations and inflections "make" the music. And rock music isn't rich harmonically, but the chords are basic blues and country chords, and they're beautiful.

Very true, and I guess I have candidly to admit that I am not terribly fond of folk music. I can be charmed by the peasant wrongheadedness of it all, and if I were a film director trying to shoot a scene in the Hebrides, let's say, I would take every modal nuance the locals had to offer, and I would not want it undercut by the sort of triadic perfection that a certain generation of Roman Catholic organists were always trying to add to the chant. But, on the other hand, I'm not very hot on Bartók and Kodaly either, who did hear in folk sounds the basis for other more sophisticated structures. Now, if that's what the Beatles did, and if you argue that they did it persuasively and with great subtlety — a subtlety that means something to you — then what can I say! I can't hear it, and I'm stubborn enough at my advanced age to say that if I can't hear it, it ain't there. But in any event, we really have struck, at this point, a generational impasse.

But the point that we were making some paragraphs back was that clarity relates to a state of mind, and it doesn't have anything to do with one idiom or one individual or one group — Steve and Eydie can have clarity if they sing in tune together, as they usually do. In any case, it isn't the private preserve of the rock scene or the jazz scene, as it was thought to be in the forties and the fifties.

Maybe it would be fair to say that your taste in pop music is a bit sentimental.

My taste in popular music? I have almost none, so I don't know if it's sentimental, but let me put it this way: I grew up with the big band sound in my head. To the extent that I could listen pleasurably to pop music, it was music that related to the harmonic spectrum of *that* sound — not that sound itself, but the harmonic spectrum to which it conformed. Now, who sings it and how well is of rather less importance to me than how inoffensively it functions as a backdrop, if that's what I'm having to listen to.

I'd say that Streisand stands to the Beatles as someone like Bellini would stand to . . . well, to almost anyone rich and variegated and intense and lively . . . like Schoenberg, for example.

That's very odd, because I would think of Streisand as being a very intense individual and a very intense artist, and I would think of Schoenberg as being an ultraintense artist and individual. There is one difference, though — Schoenberg's funny moments were pretty Germanic and

Gould as Sir Nigel Twitt-Thornwaite, the "dean
of British conductors," 1974. *(Robert C. Ragsdale,
The National Library of Canada)*

Gould in the guise of Karlheinz Klopweisser,
yet another of the pianist's fictional characters.
(Robert C. Ragsdale, The National Library of Canada)

heavy-handed, things like "*Ach, du lieber Augustine*" in the Second Quartet, whereas Streisand, obviously, is a pretty funny lady.

Well, I think my Schoenberg analogy was off. Maybe Luciano Berio is a better example.

I was going to feed you Berio. They *sure* are, they *sure* are. And I will say no more [laughing]. You've hit on a really good parallel for the Beatles.

What's the matter with Berio? . . . Oh, well . . . I've gotten myself concerned here. I should have compared the Beatles to Anton Webern.

Listen, if you had done that, I would have trotted out all my alter egos, and enlisted all my exotic *Doppelgängers*, and barraged *Rolling Stone* with a Letters-to-the-Editor campaign for the next ten years. I think I'd send my letters off to Vienna, perhaps, or to London . . . Sverdlovsk, maybe, or, for the benefit of Teddy Slotz, Brooklyn Heights. I'd get them postmarked accordingly, and they'd be coming at you indefinitely. And of course they'd all contain the same message: "This idiot Cott has done it again."

The conductor George Szell. *(CBS Records)*

THE
GEORGE SZELL
CAPER

The young Gould adjusting his famous wooden chair, 1952.
(The National Library of Canada)

Wʜᴇɴ the first of my two-part interview with Glenn Gould first appeared in *Rolling Stone* magazine in August 1974, I began my introduction as follows:

A couple of years before the Canadian pianist Glenn Gould retired from the concert stage at thirty-two, he was scheduled to rehearse Bach's *Fifth Brandenburg Concerto* with members of the Cleveland Orchestra and conductor George Szell. Out Gould came onto the stage — the musicians tuning up — and slowly a look of outraged incredulity appeared on the fastidious conductor's face.

Right under him was his debut recitalist maneuvering a little rug next to the piano, on top of which rug, methodically and intensely, the pianist began adjusting the four 3-inch screws attached to his sawed-down, short-legged, wooden folding chair, readjusting them to the height and angle that suited his exceptional performing posture — an almost on-the-floor, nose-on-the-keys slouch that has driven Victorian church-pew piano teachers into a state of total stupefaction.

Oblivious to the world but finally satisfied with the angle, Gould looked up to find that that most patriarchal of conductors, muttering indignantly, was storming off the stage, never to return in Gould's presence. An assistant conductor took over for the rehearsal, as well as for the extraordinary concert performance which Szell himself attended — sitting in the audience — and after which he turned to a friend, saying: "That nut's a genius."

As I recall, I had based my above-recounting of this legendary encounter between Gould and Szell on what I had thought were fairly well-remembered readings of several

magazine articles that had reported on Gould's debut performance with the Cleveland Orchestra in which he played
Beethoven's *Second Piano Concerto* — though I later realized that I had confused that 1957 performance with a
radio broadcast I had heard a number of years later in
which Gould had played Bach's *Fifth Brandenburg* with
that same orchestra under the direction of assistant conductor Louis Lane.

A week after the first part of the interview had appeared,
I received a telephone call from Gould, in which he thanked
me for the interview but wanted — for my interest — to
clarify the matter concerning his much-written-about encounter with George Szell. "Let me tell you the story and
in that way you'll see how much crazier it is than you
make it seem," Gould said, laughing. "Your version is by
far the mildest and most respectable that has ever appeared
in print. It's wrong, but at least it comes out in such a
way that one can read it without blushing."

The following is Gould's version of the affair:

What really happened was as follows: I had been engaged
by the Cleveland Orchestra for my first American tour —
this was in March of 1957 — and it was my Cleveland
debut. The original bill of fare was Beethoven's *Second
Piano Concerto* plus the Schoenberg *Piano Concerto*. Now,
Dr. Szell, as you well know, was awarded the Order of
Merit of the British Empire — or something like that —
for his services to British music, which consisted mainly
of giving premieres of Sir William Walton. And he had
absolutely no interest in Schoenberg or any other serious
modern music figure whatsoever. So I thought it was a

little strange that he picked the Schoenberg, but he did and that was fine. But a week before the concert, the orchestra's manager called my manager and said that Dr. Szell was much too busy with his schedule and there would not be time to rehearse the Schoenberg Concerto . . . which, translated, meant that he hadn't learned the piece, of course [laughing] — at least, that was my assumption, and I think it was a reasonable one — and that, therefore, I would just be required to do the Beethoven. Well, I wasn't about to antagonize him — I knew of his Dr. Cyclops reputation — and so, of course, I naturally agreed.

Anyway, I was at that time using the same chair that I use today, except that now it no longer even has a seat — it still did at that time, it hadn't yet been mashed up on the airlines. And I also had the little attachment for the legs. But I hadn't been able to figure out a way of getting the chair to go down an inch lower so that my legs wouldn't be positioned at a really uncomfortable trajectory. What I could do, however, was to raise the piano. And I had experimented with this at home and found it was very satisfactory.

So when I got to Cleveland, I decided that the obvious thing to do would be to have something like a block of wood with a little railing around it built for each caster of the piano, you see? So I went down to the stage. And Dr. Szell was rehearsing the *New England Triptych* by William Schuman, which was going to open the concert. The program consisted of that plus Beethoven's Second — which makes an incongruous coupling, you know, for a first half — intermission, then . . . I think it may have been

Debussy's *L'Après-Midi* — and, finally, Strauss's *Death and Transfiguration*. It was another strange coupling, but then the whole program was crazy in terms of the way it was made up. As I said, it was my debut with the orchestra, and somehow, the first time round you remember the program — when you're still a virgin, you recall it [laughing].

Anyway, I arrived at the hall and found that Dr. Szell was busy with the William Schuman. So I said to someone, "Do you have a carpenter or anyone like a carpenter who might be available who could do a little job for me on the side?" And he said, "Yeah, there's old Joe" — or whatever his name was — "down in the basement. Why don't you go down and talk to him?" So I did — he was a very nice chap — and I explained that what I wanted were blocks, which I've used ever since (not his blocks . . . I've had more sophisticated ones built, but I still use the same system because I haven't changed my seating position in all these years). So, in any event, Joe down in the basement said, "Well, I think I can do that. But what about the danger of the piano rolling off?" And I replied, "I've thought of that and I think you'll have to build a little railing around each caster." And he said, "Well, I better go up and look at that instrument." At that point, one of the assistant managers came down the basement and informed me that Dr. Szell wanted to see me onstage. And so I said to old Joe, "Look, there's obviously going to be an intermission coming up in about half an hour, and I doubt that we'll finish rehearsing at that time, probably we'll continue after it. So why don't you come up and see me during the break and we'll discuss what's to be done. And I'll just pay you your carpentry fee on the side." Because this had nothing to do with the Cleveland Orchestra, obviously.

So I went up onstage and we did the first movement of the Beethoven — everything was delightful — at the end of which the musicians had to break according to union rules. And some of the men wandered down into the hall, as orchestra musicians tend to do, and so did Szell. I don't know whether that was his habit, but I don't think so. He had a very comfortable dressing room with a chaise longue, I remember in a kind of crimson color. It was a very odd thing for Szell to have because one would have expected austere furniture and the look of Freud's studio, you know? [laughing] He had this very nice room backstage, but that day he didn't use it. He was sort of talking to the men in the first two rows, but I couldn't hear a word that was being said. And then at one point he approached the stage, the lip of the stage — he was standing, of course, below it, and therefore at shoulder height — and he said, [accent] "Vat are you doing?" And I explained that Joe and I were trying to raise the piano in lieu of lowering the chair, which had become impossible because it would not go any lower, or if it did, then my legs would be very uncomfortable indeed; but that by raising the piano, I could accomplish the same thing, and that this very kind gentleman was going to create some blocks for me which I would have ready for the evening performance. And the maestro just said, "Humm!"

He didn't say anything more, and wandered back to the collection of cronies whom he was talking to in the hall. Then after the fifteen-minute break had come to an end, the orchestra manager clapped his hands, the musicians filed back onstage, and we went back into the rehearsal, beginning with the second movement of the Beethoven. And as Szell started the tutti of the second movement — which usually takes about thirty-five seconds to get through — I realized that, while having shown the carpenter what I could do theoretically with the chair, I had unbalanced one of the little couplings down below. So I got down on the floor and, as Szell was conducting the tutti — it didn't inconvenience him in any way, by the way — I made the adjustment, put the coupling back in its proper respective relation to the other four legs of the chair — that was all — and sat down. And from there on, the rehearsal proceeded in its usual course.

I should mention — though I don't think it contributed greatly to anything that subsequently happened — that during the first movement, I had been playing with a great deal of soft pedal, as I usually do in early Beethoven (and in Mozart), in order to thin out the sound. But Szell hadn't liked that, and so he stopped conducting and said, "Excuse me, Mr. Gould, I don't understand why you are using the soft pedal. It is not necessary. It makes a very *feminine* sound." That's a quote . . . I still remember that line. And I said, "Well, Dr. Szell, I'm sure I don't need to tell you that Beethoven's piano was certainly not capable of the kind of sound this one is. And I just prefer a very thin sound with reduced climaxes, if I may say so. And if you would like me to come up a little bit, I will, but I still will do so with the soft pedal down."

So, he was a little miffed about that and obviously not at all used to being argued with, especially from a whippersnapper who was on his first American tour. However, it didn't come to blows or anything of the sort. But he did turn to Louis Lane [then assistant conductor of the Cleveland Orchestra] in the hall and shouted out something like, "Louis, can you hear enough piano?" And Louis said, "No, not quite enough." What else was Louis going to say? Louis was a very dear guy, but he was like a petrified grasshopper! I mean, he'd spent twenty years with this martinet! [laughing] So what else could he say? "Yes, not enough." Then I responded, "Listen, I'll come up a little bit. But it has really nothing to do with the soft pedal. In fact, you get a more penetrating piano sound with the soft pedal down than without it. It cuts through the textures better; it thins it out, because you're playing on two strings, of course. And it's much more appropriate for this kind of music, except in the biggest climaxes, and then I do take the pedal off. But it's just not my habit ever to play with three strings in early Beethoven, or in Mozart, or in Bach. But of course, I'll come up a little bit. That's fine."

So that was the only musical disagreement we had. And the series of concerts I gave appeared to be a great success, and Szell was very complimentary at the end of them. But he did again say, after the end of the first concert, that he still did not approve of this business of mine with the soft pedal. He thought that it was ridiculous and, once more, he told me, "I'm sorry to use the word, but it makes a very *effeminate* sound." I had the feeling that he intended a sexual connotation to this whole matter, but I pretended I didn't notice and again said, "I'm sorry you feel like that, Dr. Szell, but that's the way I play early Beethoven." What I really wanted to say to him, however, was, "Why don't you reduce some of your bloody strings! Because you've got too many of them in there!" [laughing] But, in any case, that's all there was to that.

In the meantime, I was back in Cleveland on a number of occasions, and usually played with Louis Lane when I was performing with the orchestra. But once, when I was supposed to give a solo recital, I remember that my piano, for some reason, hadn't arrived in time, and I asked for the orchestra's piano, which was a remarkably good one (they had their own Steinway which, as a house piano, was quite exceptional). And I walked over to Szell's den in Severence House, knocked on his door with temerity, went in and had a very pleasant chat. And he said that it would be fine if I used the piano for my concert. And there were a few other meetings of that kind. I ran into him once or twice in Columbia Records, for instance, and he was always very pleasant. There were no further untoward incidents at all.

Now, as you remember, in the fifties and early sixties, Szell and the Cleveland Orchestra were recording for Epic, not for Columbia. I mean, Epic *was* Columbia, but they were on Epic, which was mainly a pop and/or an import label in those days. The Juilliard Quartet was then on Epic, as was Leon Fleisher, and so was Szell. Szell wanted to be on Epic initially because it gave him the right to do, let us say, the nine Beethovens and such other material as might have been directly competitive with what Bernstein or Ormandy wanted to do at that time. And despite the fact that Szell was a far better conductor than either of the aforementioned (to me, Szell was even more accomplished than Toscanini, whose tradition he was in), his records didn't sell. They just never did. So Columbia was pushing terribly hard to get the name George Szell made into a household word. And somehow or other, they talked *Time* into doing a cover story on him — I think that was in the winter of 1963. I happened to be in Chicago at the time and picked up *Time* off the newsstand. There was George Szell on the cover, so naturally I was very curious and read the story. And I suddenly stared with horror at a particular paragraph which contained something like the following (I'll have to paraphrase this, but it's pretty close): "One of the maestro's legendary attributes is his temper which, though it does not compare with, perhaps, the late Arturo Toscanini's, runs a close second." I'm paraphrasing, but that was the gist of it. And it continued: "For example, the violinist Isaac Stern has refused to play with Szell for twenty years. Glenn Gould, the Canadian pianist, has played with him only once and has appeared on many occasions subsequently with the orchestra, but always, at the maestro's insistence, with a guest conductor. The Gould incident is typical of another facet of Szell's remarkable personality — his sparkling sense of humor . . ." [laughing] (This was not exactly one of his chief assets as far as *I* was concerned.) "During their rehearsal, Mr. Gould, a notorious eccentric who likes to fiddle with a ridiculously low piano chair, began to waste so much of the orchestra's valuable rehearsal time that the maestro, glowering down from the podium, said, 'Unless you stop that nonsense immediately, I will personally remove one-sixteenth of an inch from your derrière, thereby satisfying your need for a lower posture.'" That was essentially the quote — "one-sixteenth of an inch of your

derrière." Then they added, "Mr. Gould, in his subse-
quent visits, of course, has always been accompanied by
a guest conductor or an assistant conductor, but Dr. Szell
has, on occasion, attended his concerts and, after one,
was heard to remark, 'That nut's a genius.' " End of paragraph. On to the next story about his fabled temper. Et
cetera.

Now then, I was not only flabbergasted, I was a little
upset because nothing of the sort had ever happened. So
I called up Louis Lane, whom I knew rather well, and
said, "Listen, what is this?" And he replied, "Oh my God,
the maestro's so upset you can't imagine." Now Louis is
a very nice guy, I really like him very much, and I always
thought he was a very underrated conductor. He's an ex-
cellent conductor, but he was just so much under George
Szell's thumb that his springing to Szell's defense was, I
guess, just a conditioned reflex. But I insisted, "What's
going on? You know that never happened, Louis." And
he said, "No, of course it didn't happen. I was *there*. Good
heavens. Nothing like it ever happened." I said, "Well,
you know I just can't imagine how they would . . . I mean,
the part about fixing the chair is true, obviously. The line
about, 'that nut,' et cetera, is one that you told me yourself
years later. So *that* is true. There's enough there that's
close to something real. But how come that other thing
gets in there — that business about "I'll slice one-sixteenth
of an inch off your derrière"? And he said, "I can't imagine.
But you know the way *Time* is, they'll dig up anything."
And I said, "Well, as a matter of fact, that hasn't been
my experience. My experience is that *Time* doesn't make
up anything at all. In fact, they check so scrupulously that

they sometimes take the life out of things by their checking. They have checkers who check on the checkers, you know. They really do. And I've never had any problem with them in that way. They've been scrupulously accurate in anything they've ever written about me. And I'm really very surprised." So Louis replied, "Well, I know that if the maestro were here he'd want me to apologize, and I just can't imagine how it could have happened, nor can he. And I can assure you he's very upset; he's been talking about it all week; he just can't believe that they would print something so tasteless and totally untrue."

Okay. About a month later, Columbia asked me if I would allow *Time*'s music critic, Barry Farrell, the chap who had done the cover story on Szell, to come down and attend a recording session. And I very reluctantly did, because we normally didn't let people come to sessions. And afterwards we went out and had some tea, and then I drove him back to his office on the way up to the hotel. Nobody had mentioned the Szell thing at all, though this was only about one to two months after its appearance in print. And finally I couldn't resist and I said, "I realize this may not be a tactful question and you certainly have every right to refuse to answer — not to disclose your sources — but, as you can imagine, I'm very curious as to how you latched onto that thing about George Szell." And he said, "Well, what was that?" And I then gave him a capsule summary of what I was getting at and mentioned that a certain amount of it was certainly true: I *had* been fooling around with the chair that day, though not in such a way as to interrupt for one second his rehearsal. The "That nut's a genius" quote was told to me by Louis Lane,

which may or may not have been correct, but I don't think
Louis would have made it up. So there was a lot there
that sort of rang true. But the part that absolutely didn't
happen was any kind of fuss in front of the orchestra or
any kind of vaguely obscene comments to me. It just never
took place. And he said, "Really?" And I said, "Well, yes.
And consequently, I'd love to know who your source was.
Because somebody fed you a real line." And he said, "Well,
I guess then I can tell you. It was George Szell." And I
retorted, "You're kidding!" And he told me, "No. On my
last afternoon with him, I said, 'Dr. Szell, I seem to be
short on anecdotes that would give our readers a proper
appreciation of your sense of humor. Could you think of
one?' And this was the one he thought of." [laughing]

Now then, when Szell died in 1970, *Time* did an obit.
And they still had that anecdote in their files and they
reproduced it intact. *Newsweek* had to do a Szell story,
too; and since they couldn't appear to be copying *Time*
word for word, they, too, used but embroidered the anecdote just a little bit. I don't remember precisely the
filigree of their variation, but it was something along the
lines of: "I will *scrape* one-sixteenth of an inch off your
derrière with one of those bloody legs from your chair."
So they added that to make it seem as if they had it from
the horse's mouth, though from a different source.

Now, about three months later, out comes *Esquire* with
Martin Mayer's "Recordings" column. *Esquire* obviously
felt no restriction to be bound by what *Time* and *Newsweek*
had been bound by in terms of good taste. So Mayer went
through the usual, incorrect story about my interrupting
the rehearsal, et cetera, et cetera. And then, he com-

mented on the incredible generosity of Szell, as exempli-
fied by his habit of inviting me back year after year, despite
the fact that he personally couldn't stand me — but that
just showed what an honest and decent man he really was
despite his crochety, European manner. However, when
Mayer got to the famous moment — which, of course,
naturally happened in front of the orchestra once again,
as all these other versions had as well — he then wrote
that Dr. Szell, leering down from the podium, had said
[accent]: "Mr. Gould, if you do not stop zat nonsense
immediately, I vill personally stick . . ." — I can't remember the exact wording but it really doesn't matter —
"stick one of zose legs up your rear end."

As it happened, the managing editor of *Esquire* at that
time was an ex-Torontonian named Tom Hedley. I knew
him, and I wrote to him and said, "Look, I don't know
what the legal position on this sort of thing is, and I don't
really want to know because it's not worth it, but what I
am doing is enclosing a letter which I expect to see reprinted in full. It is only about four sentences, but I don't
want any of it cut. Not one word! And no commas changed,
either!" [laughing] And so they did, indeed, reproduce my
letter; and it was, if I may say so, a four-sentence master-
piece to the effect that the story as variated by Mr. Mayer
was, of course, based on older sources. And without both-
ering to trace all of the sources, I said it had, in substance,
been reproduced with the errors of the other magazines.
And I mentioned that I understood the generational loss
(as one spoke of it in tape-editing terms) that had gone on,
and that it had finally reached Mr. Mayer's desk undoubt-
edly in this form. However, I felt that since his obituary

was very well-intentioned as respects Dr. Szell, and since Mayer was obviously setting out to write an intensely admiring piece, it was singularly unfortunate that he chose to commemorate Dr. Szell for the one virtue that Mayer considered the conductor possessed both as a human being and as a musician, a sense of humor [laughing]. And that in so doing, moreover, Mayer had repeated something that was entirely untrue, as well as singularly tasteless. And I added that it was, of course, quite possible that this particular snappy retort, as Dr. Szell might have considered it, resided in his file of, you know, "answers-I-wish-I'd-gotten-off-at-the-time-but-forgot-to." And that over the years, it might have taken on the color of reality in his mind, as though, in fact, he *had* said it. But, I concluded, all I can tell you is that had he in *fact* said it, in front of the orchestra or to my face, the Cleveland Orchestra would have been looking for another soloist that evening. I would not have stayed around.

Anyway, the letter was a lot more snappily written than that, but that was the gist of it. *Esquire* did, indeed, publish it. And that was the end of the incident until you came along with your own variation [laughing]. So now that you know the whole story, you can make of it what you will.

APPENDICES

DISCOGRAPHY

CANADIAN
BROADCASTING CORPORATION
PRIVATE GLENN GOULD
TAPE COLLECTION

RADIO PROGRAMS

TELEVISION PROGRAMS

FILMOGRAPHY

DISCOGRAPHY

This discography derives from *The Piano Quarterly* with additions by Ruth Pincoe and CBS Records.

All titles listed are on 33-1/3rpm phonodiscs. In some Columbia releases the letter prefix *MS* indicates stereo; *ML* indicates mono.

Items are listed by composers alphabetically; works by one composer are listed alphabetically by title in English. Sometimes there are variants in the title of the same work as printed on different recordings. For example: Berg, Sonata Opus 1 and Berg, Sonata.

The year of release applies to the first release in North America only. Releases elsewhere, and rereleases in North America, are not included. The year of recording indicates that in the year mentioned Gould included among his activities the recording of part or the whole of the work listed.

Bach's *The Well-Tempered Clavier, Volumes I and II* are listed as WTC-I and WTC-II respectively.

"Trans." indicates transcribed.

With the exception of J. S. Bach, *The Art of the Fugue*, Fugues 1-9 (on organ) and G. F. Handel, Suites 1-4 (on harpsichord), musical performances by Gould are on piano.

MUSICAL PERFORMANCES BY GOULD

ANHALT, I.
>   Fantasia for Piano. Columbia Masterworks. 32110046 (stereo), 32110045 (mono) (rec. 1967, rel. 1967).

BACH, J. S.

> Art of the Fugue, Fugues 1-9. Columbia Records MS 6338, ML 5738 (rec. 1962, rel. 1962).
>
> Concerto No. 1 in D Minor. Columbia Symphony, Bernstein. Columbia Records ML 5211 (rec. 1957, rel. 1957).
>
> Concerto No. 2 in E Major. Columbia Symphony, Golschmann. Columbia Records MS 7294 (rec. 1969, rel. 1969).
>
> Concerto No. 3 in D Major. Columbia Symphony, Golschmann. Columbia Records MS 7001, ML 6401 (rec. 1967, rel. 1967).
>
> Concerto No. 4 in A Major. Columbia Symphony, Golschmann. Columbia Records MS 7294 (rec. 1969, rel. 1969).
>
> Concerto No. 5 in F Minor. Columbia Symphony, Golschmann. Columbia Records MS 7001, ML 5298 (rec. 1958, rel. 1958).
>
> Concerto No. 7 in G Minor. Columbia Symphony, Golschmann. Columbia Records MS 7001, ML 6401 (rec. 1967, rel. 1967).
>
> English Suites 1-6. Columbia Records M2 34578 (rec. 1971, 1973-76, rel. 1977).
>
> French Suites 1-4, Columbia Records M 32347 (rec. 1972-73, rel. 1973).
>
> French Suites 5, 6. Columbia Records M 32853 (rec. 1971, 1973, rel. 1974).
>
> Fugue in E Major from WTC-II. Columbia Records ML 5186 (rec. 1957, rel. 1957).
>
> Fugue in F-sharp Minor from WTC-II. Columbia Records ML 5186 (rec. 1957, rel. 1957).
>
> Goldberg Variations. Columbia Records MS 7096 (rec. 1955, rel. 1956).

BACH, J. S. (*cont.*)

Goldberg Variations. Columbia Records M 31820 (rec. 1980, rel. 1981).

Inventions and Sinfonias. Columbia Records MS 6622, ML 6022 (rec. 1963-64, rel. 1964).

Italian Concerto. Columbia Records MS 6141, ML 5472 (rec. 1959, rel. 1960).

Little Bach Book. Columbia Records M 36672 (rec. 1955, 1979, rel. 1980).

Overture in the French Style. Columbia Records M 32853 (rec. 1973, rel. 1974).

Partitas Nos. 1, 2. Columbia Records MS 6141, ML 5472 (rec. 1959, rel. 1960).

Partitas Nos. 3, 4. Columbia Records MS 6498, ML 5898 (rec. 1962-63, rel. 1963).

Partita No. 5. CBC International Service Program 120 (rec. 1954, rel. 1954).

Partitas Nos. 5, 6. Columbia Records ML 5186 (rec. 1957, rel. 1957).

Partitas for Keyboard. Columbia Records M2S 693.

Partitas, Inventions. Columbia Records D3S 754.

Preludes, Fughettas & Fugues. Columbia Records M/MT 35891 (rec. 1979, rel. 1980).

Sinfonias. (See Inventions and Sinfonias.)

Sonatas (three) for Viola da Gamba and Harpsichord. Leonard Rose, cello. Columbia Records M 32934 (rec. 1973-74, rel. 1974).

Sonatas (six) for Violin and Harpsichord. Jaime Laredo, violin. Columbia Records M2 34226 (rec. 1975-76, rel. 1976).

Toccata No. 7 in E Minor. Columbia Records MS 6498, ML 5898 (rec. 1963, rel. 1963).

Toccatas, Vol. 1. Columbia Records M/MT 35144 (rec. 1976, rel. 1979).

BACH, J. S. (*cont.*)

> Toccatas, Vol. 2. Columbia Records M/MT 35831 (rec. 1963, 1979, rel. 1980).
>
> WTC-1, Preludes and Fugues 1-8. Columbia Records MS 6408, ML 5808 (rec. 1962, rel. 1963).
>
> WTC-1, Preludes and Fugues 9-16. Columbia Records MS 6538, ML 5938 (rec. 1963, rel. 1964).
>
> WTC-I, Preludes and Fugues 17-24. Columbia Records MS 6776, ML 6176 (rec. 1965, rel. 1965).
>
> WTC-II, Preludes and Fugues 1-8. Columbia Records MS 7099 (rec. 1966-7, rel. 1968).
>
> WTC-II, Preludes and Fugues 9-16. Columbia Records MS 7409 (rec. 1969, rel. 1970).
>
> WTC-II, Preludes and Fugues 17-24. Columbia Records M 30537 (rec. 1971, rel. 1971).
>
> WTC, Bk. 1 (Complete). Columbia Records D3S 733.
>
> WTC, Bk. 2 (Complete). Columbia Records D3M 31525.
>
> Goldberg Variations. Columbia Records IM 37779 (digital) (rec. 1981, rel. 1982).

BEETHOVEN, L. V.

> Bagatelles, Op. 33, Op. 126. Columbia Records M 33265 (rec. 1974, rel. 1975).
>
> Concerto No. 1 in C Major. Columbia Symphony, Golschmann. Columbia Records Y 30491 (rec. 1958, rel. 1958).
>
> Concerto No. 2 in B-flat Major. Columbia Symphony, Bernstein. Columbia Records ML 5211 (rec. 1957, rel. 1957).
>
> Concerto No. 3 in C Minor. Columbia Symphony, Bernstein. Columbia Records MS 6096, ML 5418 (rec. 1959, rel. 1960).

Beethoven, L. v. (*cont.*)

Concerto No. 4 in C Major. New York Philharmonic, Bernstein. Columbia Records MS 6262, ML 5 ̀62 (rec. 1961, rel. 1961).

Concerto No. 5 in E-flat Major. American Symphony, Stokowski. Columbia Records MS 6888, ML 6288 (rec. 1966, rel. 1966).

Sonata No. 1 in A-flat Major, Op. 2, No. 1. Columbia Records M2 35911 (rec. 1974, 1976, rel. 1980).

Sonata No. 2 in A Major, Op. 2, No. 2. Columbia Records. M2 35911 (rec. 1974, 1976, rel. 1980).

Sonata in C Major, Op. 2, No. 3. Columbia Records M2 35911 (rec. 1976, 1979, rel. 1980).

Sonata No. 5 in C Minor, Op. 10, No. 1. Columbia Records MS 6686, ML 6086 (rec. 1964, rel. 1965).

Sonata No. 6 in F Major, Op. 10, No. 2. Columbia Records MS 6686, ML 6086 (rec. 1964, rel. 1965).

Sonata No. 7 in D Minor, Op. 10, No. 3. Columbia Records MS 6686, ML 6086 (rec. 1964, rel. 1965).

Sonata No. 8 in C Minor, Op. 13. Columbia Records MS 7413, ML 6345 (rec. 1966, rel. 1967).

Sonata No. 9 in E Major, Op. 14, No. 1. Columbia Records MS 6945, ML 6345 (rec. 1966, rel. 1967).

Sonata No. 10 in G Major, Op. 14, No. 2. Columbia Records MS 6945, ML 6345 (rec. 1966, rel. 1967).

Sonata No. 12, Op. 26. Columbia Records IM 37831 (digital) (rec. 1982, rel. 1983).

Sonata No. 13, Op. 27, No. 1. Columbia Records IM 37831 (digital) (rec. 1982, rel. 1983).

Sonata No. 14 in C-sharp Minor, Op. 27, No. 2. Columbia Records MS 7413 (rec. 1967, rel. 1970).

Sonata No. 15 in D Major, Op. 28. Columbia Records M2 35911 (rec. 1979, rel. 1980).

BEETHOVEN, L. V. (*cont.*)

Sonata No. 16 in G Major, Op. 31, No. 1. Columbia Records M 32349 (rec. 1971, 1973, rel. 1973).

Sonata No. 17 in D Minor, Op. 31, No. 2. Columbia Records M 32349 (rec. 1967, 1971, rel. 1973).

Sonata No. 18 in E-flat Major, Op. 31, No. 3. Columbia Records M 32349 (rec. 1967, rel. 1973).

Sonata No. 23 in F Minor, Op. 57. Columbia Records MS 7413 (rec. 1967, rel. 1970).

Sonata No. 30 in E Major, Op. 109. Columbia Records ML 5130 (rec. 1956, rel. 1956).

Sonata No. 31 in A-flat Major, Op. 110. Columbia Records ML 5130 (rec. 1956, rel. 1956).

Sonata No. 32 in C Minor, Op. 111. Columbia Records ML 5130 (rec. 1956, rel. 1956).

Symphony No. 5 in C Minor, trans. Liszt. Columbia Records MS 7095 (rec. 1967-68, rel. 1968).

Thirty-two Variations in C Minor. Columbia Records M 30080 (rec. 1966, rel. 1970).

Variations in E-flat Major, Op. 35. Columbia Records M 30080 (rec. 1967, 1970, rel. 1970).

Variations in F Major, Op. 34. Columbia Records M 30080 (rec. 1967, rel. 1970).

BERG, A.

Sonata Opus 1. Hallmark RS-3 (rec. 1953, rel. 1953).

Sonata. Columbia Records ML 5336 (rec. 1958, rel. 1959).

BIZET, G.

Premier Nocturne. Columbia Records M 32040 (rec. 1972, rel. 1973).

Variations Chromatiques. Columbia Records M 32040 (rec. 1971, rel. 1973).

BRAHMS, J.

> Intermezzos (ten). Columbia Records MS 6237, ML 5637 (rec. 1960, rel. 1961).
>
> Quintet in F Minor. Montreal String Quartet. CBC Transcription Service Program 140 (rec. 1957, rel. 1957).
>
> Ballades, Op. 10. Columbia Records IM 37800 (rec. 1982, rel. 1983).
>
> 2 Rhapsodies, Op. 79. Columbia Records (rec. 1982, rel. 1983).

BYRD. W.

> First Pavan and Galliard (rec. 1967), Sixth Pavan and Galliard (rec. 1967), A Voluntary (rec. 1967), Hughe Ashton's Ground (rec. 1971), Sellinger's Round (rec. 1971). Columbia Records M 30825 (rel. 1971).

GIBBONS, O.

> Allemand, or Italian Ground (rec. 1968), Fantasy in C (rec. 1968), Salisbury Pavan and Galliard (rec. 1969). Columbia Records M 30825 (rel. 1971).

GOULD, G.

> Glenn Gould Silver Jubilee Album. Side 1: 3 Scarlatti Sonatas (rec. 1968), C.P.E. Bach's (Wurttemberg) Sonata No. 1. in Am (rec. 1968), Gould, "So You Want to Write a Fugue?" (rec. 1963), Side 2: Scriabin, Two Preludes, Op. 57 (rec. 1972), Strauss, Ophelia Lieder, Op. 67 with Elisabeth Schwarzkopf (rec. 1966), Beethoven-Liszt, Symphony No. 6 in F, Op. 68 (rec. 1968), A Glenn Gould Fantasy (rec. 1980, rel. 1980), Columbia Records M2X 35914 (rel. 1980).
>
> "So You Want to Write a Fugue?" GG-101. Quartet of voices with string quartet accompaniment. Columbia Records (rec. 1963, rel. 1964).
>
> String Quartet, Op. 1. Montreal String Quartet. CBC International Service Program No. 142 (rec. 1956).

GOULD, G. (*cont.*)

    String Quartet, Op. 1. Symphonia Quartet. Columbia
        Records MS 6178, ML 5578 (rec. 1960, rel. 1960).

    Slaughterhouse-Five. Movie soundtrack. Columbia Rec-
        ords S 31333.

GRIEG, E.

    Sonata No. 7 in E Minor. Columbia Records M 32040
        (rec. 1971, rel. 1973).

HANDEL, G. F.

    Suites 1-4, Columbia Records M 31512 (rec. 1972, rel.
        1972).

HAYDN, J.

    Sonata No. 3 in E-flat Major (1789-90). Columbia Records
        ML 5274 (rec. 1958, rel. 1958).

HAYDN, F. J.

    Sonata No. 56 in D Major; Sonata No. 58 in C Major;
        Sonata No. 59 in E-flat Major; Sonata No. 60 in C
        Major; Sonata No. 61 in D Major; Sonata No. 62 in
        E-flat Major. Columbia Records I2M 36947 (digital)
        (rec. 1980, 1981-82).

HETU, J.

    Variations for Piano. Columbia Masterworks 32110046
        (stereo), 32110045 (mono) (rec. 1967, rel. 1967).

HINDEMITH, P.

    Piano Sonatas (three). Columbia Records M 32350 (rec.
        1966-67, 1973, rel. 1973).

    Sonatas (four) for Brass and Piano. Various soloists. Co-
        lumbia Records M2 33971 (rec. 1975-76, rel. 1976).

    Das Marienleben. Roxolane Roslak. Columbia Records M2
        34597.

KRENEK, E.
> Sonata No. 3. Columbia Records ML 5336 (rec. 1958, rel. 1959).

MORAWETZ, O.
> Fantaisie. CBC International Service Program 120 (rec. 1954, rel. 1969).
>
> Fantasy in D Minor. Columbia Masterworks 32110046 (stereo), 32110045 (mono) (rec. 1966, rel. 1967).

MOZART, W. A.
> Complete Piano Sonatas. Columbia Records D5S 35899.
>
> Concerto No. 24 in C Minor, K. 491. CBC Symphony, Susskind. Columbia MS 6339, ML 5739 (rec. 1961, rel. 1962).
>
> Fantasia in C Minor, K. 475. (See Fantasia and Sonata in C Minor, K.475/457).
>
> Fantasia in D Minor, K.397. Columbia Records M 32348 (rec. 1972, rel. 1973).
>
> Fantasia and Fugue in C Major, K. 394. Columbia Records ML 5274 (rec. 1958, rel. 1958).
>
> Fantasia and Sonata (no. 14) in C Minor, K.475/457. Columbia Records M 33515 (K.475, rec. 1966-67; K.457, rec. 1973-74; rel. 1975).
>
> Sonata No. 1 in C Major, K.279. Columbia Records MS 7097 (rec. 1967, rel. 1968).
>
> Sonata No. 2 in F Major, K.280. Columbia Records MS 7097 (rec. 1967, rel. 1968).
>
> Sonata No. 3 in B-flat Major, K.281, Columbia Records MS 7097 (rec. 1967, rel. 1968).
>
> Sonata No. 4 in E-flat Major, K.282. Columbia Records MS 7097 (rec. 1967, rel. 1968).
>
> Sonata No. 5 in G Major, K.283. Columbia Records MS 7097 (rec. 1967, rel. 1968).
>
> Sonata No. 6 in D Major, K.284. Columbia Records MS 7274 (rec. 1968, rel. 1969).

MOZART, W. A. (*cont.*)

> Sonata No. 7 in C Major, K.309. Columbia Records MS 7274 (rec. 1968, rel. 1969).
>
> Sonata No. 8 in A Major, K.310. Columbia Records M 31073 (rec. 1969, rel. 1972).
>
> Sonata No. 9 in D Major, K.311. Columbia Records MS 7274 (rec. 1968, rel. 1969).
>
> Sonata No. 10 in C Major, K.330. Columbia Records ML 5274 (rec. 1958, rel. 1958).
>
> Sonata No. 10 in C Major, K.330. Columbia Records M 31073 (rec. 1970, rel. 1972).
>
> Sonata No. 11 in A Major, K.331. Columbia Records M 32348 (rec. 1965, 1970, rel. 1973).
>
> Sonata No. 12 in F Major, K.332. Columbia Records M 31073 (rec. 1965-66, rel. 1972).
>
> Sonata No. 13 in B-flat Major, K.333. Columbia Records M 31073 (rec. 1970, rel. 1972).
>
> Sonata No. 14 in C Minor, K. 457. (See Fantasia and Sonata in C Minor, K.475/457).
>
> Sonata No. 15 in C Major, K.545. Columbia Records M 32348 (rec. 1967, rel. 1973).
>
> Sonata No. 16 in B-flat Major, K.570. Columbia Records M 33515 (rec. 1974, rel. 1975).
>
> Sonata No. 17 in D Major, K.576. Columbia Records M 33515 (rec. 1974, rel. 1975).
>
> Sonata in F Major with Rondo, K.533/K.494. Columbia Records M 32348 (rec. 1972-73, rel. 1973).

PROKOVIEV, S.

> Sonata No. 7 in B-flat Major, Op. 83. Columbia Records MS 7173 (rec. 1967, rel. 1969).
>
> "The Winter Fairy" (from Cinderella), trans. M. Fichten-goltz. Albert Pratz, violin. Hallmark RS-3. Columbia Records (rec. 1953, rel. 1953).

SCHOENBERG, A.

> Fantasy for Violin and Piano, Op. 47. Israel Baker, violin. Columbia Records MS 7036, ML 6436 (rec. 1964, rel. 1967).
>
> Five Piano Pieces, Op. 23. Columbia Records. MS 6817, ML 6217 (rec. 1965, rel. 1966).
>
> Ode to Napoleon Buonaparte, Op. 41. Juilliard Quartet; John Horton, speaker. Columbia Records M2S 767, ML 6437 (rec. 1965, rel. 1967).
>
> Piano Concerto, Op. 42. CBC Symphony. Craft. Columbia Records MS 6339, ML 5739 (rec. 1961, rel. 1962).
>
> Piano Pieces, Op. 33 a/b. Columbia Records MS 6817, ML 6217 (rec. 1965, rel. 1966).
>
> Six Little Piano Pieces, Op. 19. Columbia Records MS 6817, ML 6217 (rec. 1964-65, rel. 1966).
>
> Songs, Op. 1, 2, 15. Donald Gramm, bass-baritone; Ellen Faull, soprano; Helen Vanni, mezzo-soprano. Columbia Records MS 6816, ML 6216 (rec. 1964-65, rel. 1966).
>
> Songs, Op. 3, 6, 12, 14, 48, Op. Posth. Donald Gramm, bass-baritone; Cornelis Opthof, baritone; Helen Vanni, mezzo-soprano. Columbia Records M 31312 (rec. 1964-65, 1968, 1970-71, rel. 1972).
>
> Suite for Piano, Op. 25. Columbia Records MS 6817, ML 6217 (rec. 1964, rel. 1966).
>
> Three Piano Pieces, Op. 11. Columbia Records ML 5336 (rec. 1958, rel. 1959).

SCHUMANN, R.

> Quartet in E-flat Major for Piano and Strings. Juilliard Quartet. Columbia Records D3S 806, (rec. 1968, rel. 1969).

SCRIABIN, A.

> Sonata No. 3. Columbia Records MS 7173 (rec. 1968, rel. 1969).

SHOSTAKOVITCH, D.

> Three Fantastic Dances, trans. H. Glickman. Albert Pratz, violin. Hallmark RS-3 (rec. 1953, rel. 1953).

SIBELIUS, J.

> Three Sonatinas, Op. 67; Kyllikki, Three Lyric Pieces for Piano, Op. 41. Columbia Records M 34555 (rec. 1977, rel. 1977; mixed 1977).

STRAUSS, R.

> Enoch Arden. Claude Rains, speaker. Columbia Records MS 6341, ML 5741. (rec. 1961, rel. 1962).
>
> Five Pieces, Op. 3. Columbia Records M 38659 (rec. 1982, rel. 1983).
>
> Piano Sonata, Op. 5. Columbia Records M 38659 (rec. 1982, rel. 1984).
>
> Sonata in B Minor; Five Pieces, Op. 3. Columbia Records M 38659 (rec. 1982, rel. 1984).

TANEIEFF, S.

> "The Birth of the Harp." trans. A. Hartmann. Albert Pratz, violin. Hallmark RS-3 (rec. 1953, rel. 1953).

WAGNER, R.

> Three transcriptions by Gould: Die Meistersinger, "Prelude;" "Dawn and Siegfried's Rhine Journey" from Die Gotterdammerung; Siegfried Idyll. Columbia Records M 32351 (rec. 1973, rel. 1973).

Canadian Broadcasting Corporation Private Glenn Gould Tape Collection

The following is a listing from the Canadian Broadcasting Corporation of its special tape collection of performances recorded by Glenn Gould between 1951 and 1957.

The date listed is the date the recording was made. The archive number corresponds to the CBC's cataloging system for this material; unavailable archive numbers are designated unknown.

March 6, 1951, archive no. unknown. Konzertstück, by Carl Weber. Toronto Symphony Orchestra, conducted by Sir Ernest MacMillan.

October 28, 1951, archive no. 6728(18). *Vancouver Symphony Orchestra* series: Piano Concerto No. 4 in G, by Beethoven (incomplete — sides 2 and 4 only of original discs), conducted by William Steinberg. (Sound very poor.)

September 28, 1952, archive no. 6728(12). *Distinguished Artists* series: Variations in F on an Original Theme, Opus 34, by Beethoven. Set of 6 Bagatelles, Opus 126, by Beethoven.

October 12, 1952, archive no. 6728(8). *CBC Conert:* Sonata No. 4 in E Flat, Opus 7, by Beethoven. Sonata No. 28 in A, Opus 101, by Beethoven.

October 14, 1952, archive no. 6728(15). *CBC Concert Hall* series: Piano Sonata, Opus 1, by Alban Berg. Suite for Piano, Opus 25, by Arnold Schoenberg.

October 21, 1952, archive no. 6728(9). *CBC Concert Hall* series: Fantasia for Organ (arranged for piano solo), by Jan Pieterszoon Sweelinck. Italian Concerto (transcribed for piano), by J. S. Bach.

December 21, 1953, archive no. 6728(14). *CBC Symphony Orchestra* series: Concerto for Piano and Orchestra, by Arnold Schoenberg. Conducted by Jean Beaudet.

February 28, 1954, archive no. 6728(6). *Distinguished Artists* series: Prelude and Fugue in F Sharp, from Volume II of the Well-Tempered Clavier, by J. S. Bach. Five Sinfonias (three-part inventions) in E, F, G, B Flat, and D, by J. S. Bach. Prelude and Fugue in E Flat and Prelude and Fugue in B Flat, from Volume II of the Well-Tempered Clavier, by J. S. Bach.

June 7, 1954, archive no. 6728(10). *Distinguished Artists* series: Sinfonia in A (or three-part invention), by J. S. Bach. Partita No. 5 in G, by J. S. Bach. Fugue in C from Ludus Tonalis, by Paul Hindemith.

June 7, 1954, archive no. 6728(11). *Distinguished Artists* series (continued from 6728[10]): Piano Sonata No. 3, by Paul Hindemith.

July 18, 1954, archive no. 6728(7). *Summer Festival* (TV series): Trio in B Flat, by Beethoven. Trio in D, No. 1, Opus 70, by Beethoven. Alexander Schneider, violin; Zara Nelsova, cello.

December 16, 1954, archive no. 6728(20). *TV Concert Hour* series: Piano Concerto No. 1 (first movement only), by Beethoven. Conducted by Paul Scherman.

February 21, 1955, archive no. 88341. *CBC Symphony Orchestra* series: Concerto No. 3 in C for Piano and Orchestra, by Beethoven. Conducted by Dr. Heinz Unger.

March 29, 1955, archive no. 6728(16). *Toronto Symphony Orchestra* series: Concerto No. 1 in D for Clavier and String Orchestra, by J. S. Bach. Conducted by Sir Ernest MacMillan.

October 19, 1955, archive no. 6728(17). *CBC Wednesday Night* series: Sonata No. 32 in C, Opus 111, by Beethoven.

January 17, 1956, archive no. 96527. *CBC Concert Hall* series: The Pavan and Gaillard of the Lord of Salisbury from Pieces for the Virginal, by Orlando Gibbons. Partita in 3, No. 6, by J. S. Bach.

October 23, 1956, 6728(19). *Toronto Symphony Orchestra* series: Piano Concerto No. 2 in B Flat, by Beethoven. Conducted by Walter Susskind.

May 26, 1957, archive no. 6728(4). Concerto No. 3 for Piano and Orchestra, 1st and 2nd movements (3rd on 6728[5]), by Beethoven. Berlin Philharmonic Orchestra.

May 26, 1957, archive no. 6728(5). Concerto No. 3 for Piano and Orchestra, 3rd movement. Berlin Philharmonic Orchestra.

Undated, archive no. 6728(1). Concerto No. 2 in B Flat, Opus 19, by Beethoven. CBC Little Symphony Orchestra, conducted by Roland Leduc.

Undated, archive no. 6728(2). See 6728(6), February 28, 1954.

Undated, archive no 6728(3), Variations for Piano, Opus 27, by Anton Webern. Concerto No. 2 for Piano and Orchestra, 3rd movement (Rondo), by Beethoven.

Undated, archive no. 6728(13). Sinonias by Bach: No. 3 in D; No. 4 in D; No. 8 in F; No. 9 in F; Fugue in F sharp (No. 14) from the Well-Tempered Clavichord (Book 2); No. 1 in C; No. 2 in C; No. 5 in E Flat; No. 14 in B Flat; No. 11 in G; No. 10 in G; No. 15 in B; No. 7 in E; No. 6 in E; No. 12 in A; No. 13 in A.

RADIO PROGRAMS

Following is a selected list of radio programs Glenn Gould produced for the Canadian Broadcasting Corporation. The year given is that of the original broadcast.

Arnold Schoenberg: The Man Who Changed Music (1962). Documentary on the life and works of Arnold Schoenberg.

The Prospects of Recording (1965). Documentary study of the recording industry and the effect of recordings on the life of modern man.

Psychology of Improvisation (1966). Documentary on the nature of improvisation in music.

The Art of Glenn Gould (first series, 1966/67). An eleven-program series featuring recordings of Glenn Gould and including the documentary "On Records and Recording."

Conference at Point Chilkoot (1967). .A critical study of music critics and criticism presented in the form of a dramatic dialogue.

Search for Petula Clark (1967). Documentary on radio, Northern Ontario, and popular music based on Gould's article.

The Idea of North (1967). Documentary on life in the Canadian North; Gould's first experiment with contrapuntal radio.

Anti Alea (1968). Documentary; on the idea of chance.

The Art of Glenn Gould (second series, 1969). A twenty-one-program series featuring recordings of Glenn Gould combined with documentary material and interviews.

The Latecomers (1967). Documentary on life in the Newfoundland outparts.

Stokowski: A Portrait for Radio (1971). Documentary on the life and music of Leopold Stokowski.

The Scene (1972). In the format of a sports report, Gould and Harry Brown debate the value of games, competitive sport, and the effect of technology on art.

The Quiet in the Land (1973). Documentary on a Mennonite community.

Casals: A Portrait for Radio (1974). Documentary on the life and music of Pablo Casals.

Schoenberg Centennial Documentary Series (1974). A ten-program series featuring the music and ideas of Arnold Schoenberg.

Schoenberg: The First 100 Years (1974). Documentary/fantasy on Arnold Schoenberg.

Richard Strauss: The Bourgeois Hero (1979). Documentary on the life and works of Richard Strauss.

TELEVISION PROGRAMS

Following is a selected list of television programs Glenn Gould produced for the Canadian Broadcasting Corporation. The year given is that of the original broadcast.

The Subject Is Beethoven (1961). A documentary/recital.

Music in the U.S.S.R. (1962). Documentary on the development of Russian music. Includes performances by Gould of works by Shostakovich and Prokofiev.

Anatomy of a Fugue (1963). A documentary on the fugue. *So You Want to Write a Fugue?* was composed for the finale.

Conversations with Glenn Gould (1966). A series of four interviews with Humphrey Burton on Bach, Beethoven, Richard Strauss, Schoenberg.

The World of Music (1968). Glenn Gould introduces a series of six television specials ("I Solisti di Zagreb"; "Majesty in Mantua"; "The Boston Symphony at Tanglewood"; "Von Karajan conducts the *New World Symphony*"; "Messaien and Willan"; "Mozart's *Abduction from the Seraglio*.")

Well-Tempered Listener (1970). Glenn Gould, interviewed by Curtis Davis, on Bach and his music.

The Idea of North (1970). Documentary on life in the Canadian North, based on the CBC Radio program and featuring Glenn Gould's first experiment with contrapuntal radio.

Glenn Gould's Toronto (from the series *Cities*) (1979). Glenn
Gould presents his view of Toronto.

Sound or Unsound (number 8 of the series *Music of Man*) (1979).
A documentary on the diversity of developments in music
since World War II. Includes Glenn Gould in conversation
with Yehudi Menuhin on the relative merits of live and recorded music and shows Gould supervising a remix in a recording studio.

FILMOGRAPHY

Glenn Gould On the Record and *Glenn Gould Off the Record* (both 1959). Documentary films on Glenn Gould. National Film Board of Canada.

Conversations with Glenn Gould (1966). Four films of conversations between Gould and Humphrey Burton on Beethoven, Strauss, Schoenberg, and Bach. British Broadcasting Corporation.

Spheres (1969). Animated film by Norman McLaren and Rene Jodoin, using music by J. S. Bach played by Glenn Gould, as musical soundtrack. National Film Board.

Slaughterhouse-Five (1972). Feature film, based on a novel by Kurt Vonnegut, Jr., directed by George Roy Hill; musical soundtrack arranged and performed by Glenn Gould. Universal Pictures.

Music and Technology, Chemins de la Musique (1973-76). Series of four films made by Bruno Monsaingeon, featuring Glenn Gould talking about and performing music by Bach, Schoenberg, Scriabin, Gibbons, Byrd, Berg, and Wagner. O.R.T.F. (I.N.A.)

The Terminal Man (1974). Feature film, based on a novel by Michael Crichton, directed by Michael Hodges; musical soundtrack is *Goldberg Variations*, played by Glenn Gould. Warner Brothers.

Radio As Music (1975). Film adaptation of an article by John Jessop (in collaboration with Gould) on Glenn Gould's contrapuntal radio documentary techniques.

Bach Series (1979-81). Series of three films of Glenn Gould talking about and performing the music of Bach: *Goldberg Variations, Chromatic Fantasy, Partita No. 4,* and excerpts from *The Well-Tempered Clavier* and *Art of the Fugue.* Clasart.

The Wars (1983). Feature film, based on the novel by Timothy Findley, directed by Robin Philips; musical soundtrack arranged and performed by Glenn Gould.

Variations on Glenn Gould. Profile/documentary on Glenn Gould at a recording session; making a radio documentary; and in the Ontario northland.

ABOUT THE AUTHOR

Jonathan Cott was educated at Columbia College, the University of California, Berkeley, and the University of Essex in England. He is the author of *Stockhausen: Conversations with the Composer*; *He Dreams What Is Going On inside His Head*, a collection of essays, interviews, and reviews; *City of Earthly Love*, a collection of poems; *Forever Young*, a collection of interviews; *Pipers at the Gates of Dawn*, a collection of interview-essays with creators and scholars of children's literature; and *Bob Dylan*, a critical biography of the songwriter. He has also edited *The Roses Race around Her Name: Poems from Fathers to Daughters*; *Beyond the Looking Glass: Victorian Fairy Tale Novels, Stories and Poems*; and the seven-volume *Masterworks of English Children's Literature: 1550-1900*. He has also coedited *Wonders*, a collection of writings for children and adults, and *The Ballad of John & Yoko*. His poetry had been widely anthologized and has appeared in such places as the *Paris Review* and the *American Poetry Review*. He is a contributing editor of *Rolling Stone*, and his articles have been published there for the last sixteen years, as well as in the *New York Times*, *American Review*, and *The New Yorker*.